MALAYSIA
in Pictures

Francesca Di Piazza

TF
CB
Twenty-First Century Books

Contents

Twenty-First Century Books
A division of Lerner Publishing Group
241 First Avenue North
Minneapolis, MN 55401 U.S.A.

Website address: www.lernerbooks.com

web enhanced @ www.vgsbooks.com

Library of Congress Cataloging-in-Publication Data

Di Piazza, Francesca.
    Malaysia in pictures / by Francesca Di Piazza.—Rev. & expanded.
        p.   cm. — (Visual geography series)
    Includes bibliographical references and index.
    ISBN-13: 978-0-8225-2674-2 (lib. bdg. : alk. paper)
    ISBN-10: 0-8225-2674-3 (lib. bdg. : alk. paper)
    1. Malaysia—Juvenile literature. I. Title. II. Visual geography series
    (Minneapolis, Minn.)
DS592.05 2006
959.5—dc22   2005017430

Manufactured in the United States of America
1 2 3 4 5 6 - BP - 11 10 09 08 07 06

INTRODUCTION

Malaysia is a country in Southeast Asia. This region of the globe is near the equator, the halfway point between the North Pole and the South Pole. Southeast Asia is bounded by the Indian Ocean on the west and the Pacific Ocean on the east. Southeast Asia also includes the countries of Myanmar, Laos, Thailand, Vietnam, Cambodia, Brunei, the island nations of Singapore, Indonesia, and the Philippines, and other island nations.

The South China Sea divides Malaysia into two parts, the peninsular mainland and the northern part of the island of Borneo. Forested mountains and swampy coastal plains dominate Malaysia's landscape. Tropical rain forests grow abundantly in Malaysia's hot and humid climate. The land is rich in natural resources, including rubber, tin, timber, and tropical fruits. The seacoasts provide ports for fishing and international trade shipping. Plentiful inland rivers provide fish, water for agriculture, and transportation routes.

The wealth of Malaysia's land has attracted people throughout the nation's history. Early peoples lived in caves more than forty thousand

years ago. Migrants arrived over the centuries, and in about A.D. 1400, Malay-speaking peoples established a wealthy trading kingdom based in Melaka, a port city on a key shipping route. The lucrative trade in Asian spices and other valuable goods eventually attracted European powers. In 1511 the Portuguese captured Melaka and held it until the Dutch seized it in 1641. The British, in turn, rose to prominence in Malaysia in the late 1700s. By the early 1900s, the British Empire, which controlled 25 percent of the world's resources, had gained control over all of modern-day Malaysia. The land was called British Malaya.

Under the British, the country developed economically, and many immigrants from China and India arrived to work in tin mines and rubber plantations. The British built a strong infrastructure, or system of public works, such as roads. During World War II (1939–1945), the Japanese drove the British out and occupied Malaya. After the defeat of the Japanese and the end of the war, a Chinese Malaysian Communist uprising known as the Emergency kept the British in a state of war.

Malaysia

- ⊕ Capital city
- ● City
- ■ National park/ Wildlife refuge
- ■ Point of interest
- — International border
- — State border

0 150 KM
0 150 Miles

N

THAILAND

PERLIS
LANGKAWI
KEDAH
Alor Setar
Chenderoh
Lake
Chenderoh
PENANG
George Town
Taiping
Tumpat
KELANTAN
Ipoh
PERAK
TERENGGANU
Kuala Terengganu
Shah Alam
Klang
Putrajaya
Batu Caves
Kuala Lumpur
SELANGOR
PAHANG
Taman Negara National Park
NEGERI SEMBILAN
MELAKA
Melaka
JOHOR
Endau Rompin National Park
Johor Baharu
SINGAPORE
Johor Strait

SUMATRA

INDONESIA

Equator

Kuching
Semenggoh Wildlife Rehabilitation Centre
BORNEO
SARAWAK
Bintulu
Niah Caves National Park
BRUNEI
Kota Kinabalu
SABAH

South China Sea

Sulu Sea

Celebes Sea

Strait of Malacca

INDIAN OCEAN
INDIA
CAMBODIA
MYANMAR
LAOS
VIETNAM
THAILAND
CHINA
Taiwan
PHILIPPINES
JAPAN
PACIFIC OCEAN
INDONESIA
AUSTRALIA

0 1000 KM
0 1000 Miles

But the nation worked toward independence mostly through peaceful political means and achieved it in 1957.

Modern Malaysia has been shaped most by Prime Minister Mahathir Mohamed, who came to power in 1981. Under his guidance, Malaysia went from an economy that relied on natural products (such as rubber) to an industrialized economy that specialized in manufacturing electronics and high-technology components. Mahathir also championed the rights of ethnic Malays. The nation's prosperity eased the tensions between different ethnic groups. Mahathir's strong leadership also ensured that the gradual rise of Islam as a political force has generally been peaceful. In 2003 Mahathir resigned as prime minister and was followed by his chosen successor, Abdullah Badawi. Prime Minister Abdullah has promised to keep Malaysia on the track of economic and democratic development and ethnic and religous harmony.

Almost 26 million people live in Malaysia. The nation's people are a diverse group of ethnicities, religions, and languages. The Malays and the native peoples of Borneo—the descendants of the original peoples of prehistoric times—are called *bumiputras*, or "people of the soil." Under British rule, Malaysia encouraged large numbers of Chinese and Indian people to come and work. In modern Malaysia, many Indonesians come to Malaysia as migrant workers. These different groups tend to maintain their separate religions, cultures, languages, and even occupations. Malays, who are mostly Muslim, are dominant in politics. The Chinese, who follow Buddhism and other Asian religions, dominate Malaysia's economic sectors. Indian Malaysians are mostly Hindus and work as laborers and merchants. Many of the people of Borneo follow traditional ways of life in the rain forests, farming and hunting and practicing Christianity or the religions of their ancestors. Tensions have occasionally flared up between the country's different groups, but Malaysia is largely a peaceful, prosperous, and pleasant land.

THE LAND

Malaysia lies just north of the equator in Southeast Asia. The nation can be divided geographically into two parts. Peninsular Malaysia, or West Malaysia, contains eleven states and two federally administered cities, Kuala Lumpur and Putrajaya. West Malaysia occupies the southern third of the narrow Malay Peninsula and many nearby islands. The other part of Malaysia is known as East Malaysia. It consists of two additional states, Sarawak and Sabah, that take up most of the northern coast of the large island of Borneo. At their nearest point, West and East Malaysia are separated by 400 miles (640 kilometers) of the South China Sea.

Thailand borders West Malaysia in the northwest. The island nation of Singapore lies just across the Johor Strait in the south. The Indonesian island of Sumatra lies across the Strait of Malacca to the west. The entire east coast of West Malaysia borders the South China Sea. East Malaysia shares the island of Borneo—the world's third-largest island after Greenland and New Guinea—with two other

countries. The Indonesian province of Kalimantan makes up the southern two-thirds of the island. The tiny, oil-rich nation of Brunei shares the northern coast with Sarawak.

The total area of Malaysia is 127,320 square miles (329,758 sq. km), a little larger than New Mexico. West Malaysia accounts for about 40 percent of the country's total area and stretches for a distance of about 460 miles (736 km) from north to south. At its widest point, West Malaysia is slightly over 200 miles (320 km) wide. East Malaysia contains about 60 percent of Malaysia's land area. It extends approximately 700 miles (1,130 km) in length from the west end of the state of Sarawak to the easternmost point of the state of Sabah.

Topography

A single series of mountains dominates the topography of both portions of Malaysia. A chain of several different ranges makes up the mountains. This chain begins in Myanmar, continues to the tip of

West Malaysia, dips under the South China Sea, and reappears on the island of Borneo. The mountains consist of granite ridges that rose millions of years ago when the earth's crust pushed upward and folded onto itself. The coastal plains that surround these regions are narrow and often swampy. They eventually give way to lush tropical rain forests that grow on the mountainsides.

Despite the greenness of its vegetation, Malaysia does not have very fertile land. Heavy rains rob the soil of many of its nutrients, making it more suitable for specialized export crops (such as rubber and palm oil) than for growing vegetables or grains.

West Malaysia

Four major mountain ranges exist in West Malaysia. In the west, the Bintang Range runs southward from Thailand to the Larut Hills near the Malaysian city of Taiping. Just east of the Bintang Range is the Titi Wangsa Range, the longest stretch of high country in West Malaysia. Visible from the capital city of Kuala Lumpur, this range contains many summits that reach heights of 6,000 feet (1,830 meters) above sea level. A third chain, the Mount Tahan Range, rises in the central region and runs southeastward almost to the Pahang River valley. At that point, the mountains level out into a series of highland plains that continue to the southern end of the peninsula. The range takes its name from Mount Tahan, which at 7,175 feet (2,187 m) is West Malaysia's highest peak. The Timor Range is the easternmost of the four mountain chains. It runs along the upper two-thirds of Malaysia's peninsula.

Coastal plains flank West Malaysia. Mangrove swamps and mud flats fringe the western coastal plain, which is 50 miles (80 km) wide in most places. Mangrove trees have partly aboveground roots and can live in salty water. This coastal region also supports the largest population and the greatest economic activity. The narrower eastern coastal plain consists of broad, sandy beaches formed by the pounding of the rough South China Sea.

East Malaysia

The great mountain chain that sinks underneath the South China Sea at the tip of the Malay Peninsula resurfaces on the island of Borneo as a group of mountain ranges. These ranges run from west to east. In far western Sarawak, these mountains rise close to the seacoast. They rarely exceed 5,000 feet (1,525 m). Through most of Sarawak, the mountains begin about 60 miles (96 km) inland from the coast. The most spectacular of Borneo's mountain chains, the Crocker Range rises in western Sabah and extends northeastward.

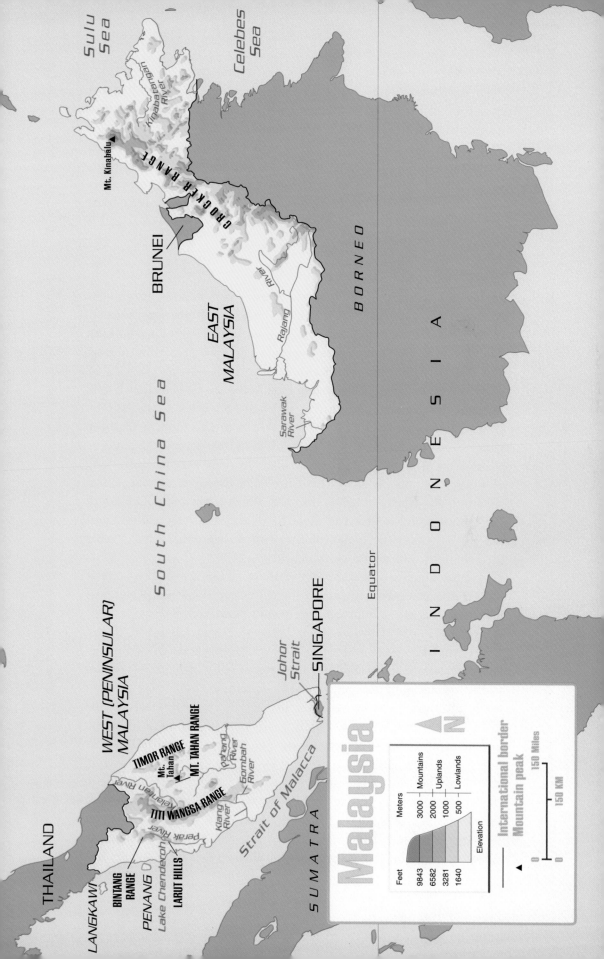

Malaysia

Sulu Sea

Celebes Sea

Kinabatangan River

Mt. Kinabalu ▲

CROCKER RANGE

BRUNEI

BORNEO

EAST MALAYSIA

River

River

Rajang

South China Sea

Sarawak River

THAILAND

LANGKAWI

BINTANG RANGE

PENANG

LARUT HILLS

Perak River

Lake Chenderoh

Kelantan River

TIMOR RANGE

Mt. Tahan

MT. TAHAN RANGE

WEST (PENINSULAR) MALAYSIA

Pahang River

TITI WANGSA RANGE

Gombak River

Klang River

Strait of Malacca

SUMATRA

Johor Strait

SINGAPORE

Equator

I N D O N E S I A

Elevation

Feet	Meters	
9843	3000	Mountains
6582	2000	Uplands
3281	1000	
1640	500	Lowlands

International border

▲ Mountain peak

N

0 — 150 KM
0 — 150 Miles

Near the eastern end of this range stands Mount Kinabalu (13,431 ft., or 4,094 m). This is Malaysia's highest peak and the highest peak in Asia southeast of the Himalayas.

The plain between Borneo's mountains and its northern coast is often narrow. But some portions of it reach 50 miles (80 km) wide, especially in central Sarawak. Estuaries (where ocean tides meet river currents) indent Sarawak's swampy coast. The eastern coast of Sabah, on the Sulu and Celebes seas, is also very irregular and is marked by a number of bays.

Bodies of Water

Malaysia's year-round rains create many rivers and streams across Malaysia. The longest rivers—the Rajang and the Kinabatangan—flow through East Malaysia. Both rivers travel 350 miles (560 km). They provide valuable routes for trade and transportation in interior regions, where few roads exist.

In the mountains, the rivers in East Malaysia flow straightly and quickly, but they move slowly through the coastal plains. The water carries sediments that often collect at the mouths of these rivers, forming swampy deltas where mangrove forests develop.

In West Malaysia, the longest waterway is the 205-mile-long (330 km) Pahang. It flows east into the South China Sea. The Kelantan River also empties into the South China Sea. The Perak River runs into the Strait of Malacca. Malay villages—called kampongs—lie along the banks of the peninsula's waterways. Rivers provide both transportation and fish.

Very few lakes of any great size exist in Malaysia. The largest, Lake Chenderoh, is artificial. It formed when the Perak River was dammed to create a hydroelectric power plant.

Climate

Because Malaysia is located near the equator, very little change occurs in the average daily temperature. The equator is the hottest zone on earth. Daytime highs in Malaysia are usually in the low 90s°F (low 30s°C). Nighttime lows are usually in the mid-70s°F (low 20s°C). The highest temperature ever recorded in West Malaysia was 102°F (39°C).

Near the equator, days and nights remain close to equal length all year long. This helps maintain steady temperatures. For links to weather reports in Malaysia and to photos and information about its cities, national parks, and more, go to www.vgsbooks.com.

Across the **Strait of Malacca,** the sun nears the horizon.

The lowest recorded temperature—taken in the Titi Wangsa Range—was 36°F (2°C). Altitude moderates the temperatures. In Malaysia's high country, days range from slightly cool to pleasantly warm, and nights are chilly enough to make jackets and warm blankets necessary.

Malaysia is a wet country. The annual average rainfall on the peninsula is 100 inches (250 centimeters). An average of 150 inches (380 cm) of rain falls every year on East Malaysia. Rarely a day passes without at least a brief downpour, but it usually doesn't rain all day long. Daily humidity levels are quite high, usually close to 90 percent, creating a sticky, heavy feeling in the air. Rainfall intensifies during Malaysia's two rainy seasons—from November to April and from May to October. The drenching rains are brought by a monsoon. This seasonal wind usually blows across a large expanse of ocean. The wind gathers water vapor, which comes down as rain.

The hibiscus is Malaysia's national flower, but it has been a popular garden flower all over the world for hundreds of years. Arabic sources mention hibiscus being cultivated as far away as Spain in the twelfth century.

Flora and Fauna

Malaysia's warm, wet climate supports thick and varied vegetation. At least twenty thousand species of flowering plants flourish, including many kinds of tropical fruits. The national flower is the hibiscus. Tropical forests cover about 78,000 square miles (202,020 sq. km)—60 percent—of Malaysia. Scientists have identified more than three thousand species of trees in these forests, with more yet to be cataloged. Malaysia's forests consist primarily of hardwood trees such as mahogany, which can grow as tall as 150 feet (46 m). A few stands of pine, a softwood, grow in the hills. Palm trees appear near rivers or villages, where the competition for sunlight is not as fierce as it is in the thick forests.

The rafflesia is the world's largest flower. Its blooms are up to 3 feet (1 m) wide and weigh as much as 20 pounds (9 kilograms). The plant is a parasite that feeds on the roots of forest trees. The beauty of its pink and red flowers is not matched by their scent. The rafflesia attracts flies by smelling like rotten meat.

Rain forests have sparse vegetation at ground level because the branches of tall trees form a leafy canopy (roof) that allows little light to filter through to shorter species. Thick vines called lianas climb the trees to find sunlight in the upper reaches of the forest. Other plants called epiphytes, or air plants, find rootholds on upper tree branches. They send down slender supporting stems that gather moisture directly from the humid air. Malaysia's many kinds of wild orchids are epiphytes.

Malaysia is home to an astonishing variety of wild animals. The endangered Malaysian tiger is the country's national animal. The two-horned rhinoceros was once common but has become extremely rare. A few thousand Asian elephants still inhabit Malaysia's forests along with a small number of leopards and other wild cats. Malaysia's only bear is the sun bear, named for its yellow chest. Otters, catlike civets, water buffalo, wild oxen, and deer are common animals. The tapir is a hoofed animal with a stubby trunk. Its black-and-white coloring provides camouflage in the shadowy forest. Pangolins, or scaly anteaters, roll up in balls for protection. Wild pigs rummage through the forest for fallen fruits and nuts and even climb into the lower branches of trees to reach food. Monkeys are a common sight in Malaysia, even near cities. There are ten different species, including the proboscis monkey. Its name comes from its long, bulblike proboscis, or nose. Flying squirrels are active at night, gliding high in the forest canopy. More than one hundred kinds of bats eat mostly insects. Fruit bats, however, feed on fruit and nectar. Also known as flying foxes, fruit bats are the world's largest bats.

Reptiles abound in Malaysia, with 250 species and more than 100 kinds of snakes, including cobras, vipers, and pythons. So-called flying snakes appear to be flying as they use a special flap of loose skin to slide between forest trees. Monitor lizards, flesh-eating reptiles, grow up to 7 feet (2 m) long. Crocodiles are riverbank and swamp dwellers. Sea turtles lay their eggs on offshore islands.

More than 150,000 species of insects thrive in Malaysia, including ants, termites, mosquitoes, and hundreds of kinds of butterflies. The moon moth is one of the most beautiful insects, with green coloring and long tail streamers.

The **green turtle** is one of the four kinds of sea turtles in the world that lay eggs on Malaysia's beaches. All four species are endangered.

The **hornbill** of southern Asia is distinguished by the bony, bright yellow helmet, or casque, on its head.

Hundreds of bird species inhabit Malaysia. Birds of prey include the crested serpent eagle and the bat hawk, which eats bats. Water birds include sandpipers, storks, and herons. The Oriental darter catches fish by stabbing them with its daggerlike beak. The rain forest's eight kinds of hornbills have big, down-curving bills. Hornbills are one of the country's main attractions for bird-watchers.

Natural Resources and Environmental Concerns

Malaysia has a wealth of natural resources. Its mineral riches include tin, petroleum (crude oil), natural gas, copper, and iron ore. Its tropical forests produce rubber, timber, and palm oil. Farmers grow rice, cacao beans (source of cocoa), pepper, coconuts, and pineapples and other tropical fruits. Coastal waters supply fish and seafood such as shrimp. Rushing rivers are harnessed for hydroelectric power. Waterways also provide transportation, and the seacoasts host major ports that connect Malaysia to international trade.

Industrial growth has helped Malaysia's economy, but it has also created serious challenges for the country's environment. Industrial waste, raw sewage, and soil runoff create high levels of water pollution. Scientists determine that only 28 percent of Malaysia's rivers are unpolluted. Damming rivers to create power plants has drowned large tracts of forest and has forced many indigenous (native) peoples from their homes. Industry and car and truck emissions cause heavy air pollution.

Malaysia's air quality also suffers from polluting haze caused by forest fires set in nearby Indonesia. Indonesian farmers and miners set most of them to clear land every year. A haze from the fires' dense smoke hangs in the air for more than one month at a time as it drifts over Malaysia. In summer 2005, air pollution from the haze reached the danger zone. Many people who had to go outside wore face masks. The Malaysian and Indonesian governments are working together to solve the ongoing problem.

The uncontrolled harvesting of trees is a major concern in Malaysia. Logging too rapidly without replanting trees has resulted in rapid deforestation (loss of forest). About 60 percent of Malaysia's rain forest has been cut down for logs or to clear land for agriculture. Without trees to hold soil in place, soil washes into rivers, polluting the water. The government has created national parks on the peninsula, and Malaysia's marine parks protect underwater environments. But the forests of Sabah and Sarawak are not protected. Due to habitat loss and hunting, 124 species of Malaysia's animals and 681 species of its plants are threatened or endangered, and many forest-dwelling people are losing their traditional ways of life.

THE FOREST PERSON

Orangutan—the Malay name for the large, orange-haired ape—means "forest person," and these shy, gentle animals have many peoplelike characteristics. The orangutan is the only great ape in Asia. It lives in the wild only on the islands of Sumatra and Borneo. Unlike other apes, the solitary orangutan spends most of its life in the trees. Each night, the ape builds a nest of sticks in a tree to sleep in. An old saying has it that these powerful and agile animals could swing from branch to branch across Borneo and never touch the ground. However, deforestation has made this impossible, and orangutans have become an endangered species. There are four orangutan sanctuaries (protected places) in the world, including the Semenggoh Wildlife Rehabilitation Centre on Sarawak. This center takes care of orangutans, monkeys, and other orphaned or illegally captured animals.

Many scientists believe that the loss of forests, which produce oxygen for the planet, increases global warming. Global warming is the gradual increase in the earth's temperature. Scientists have argued that carbon dioxide from vehicles, power plants, and industry also upsets the balance of gases in the earth's atmosphere and contributes to this warming trend.

Cities

While many Malaysians live in kampongs, the country has several modern, large cities. About 62 percent of the population lives in urban areas.

KUALA LUMPUR, the nation's capital, has a population of 1.4 million. Often called KL, the city lies on the western side of West Malaysia, where the Klang and the Gombah rivers meet. This location gave Kuala Lumpur its name, which means "muddy river junction" in the Malay language. Built in the mid-1800s as a tin-mining town, KL is the commercial center of Malaysia. On the southern edge of KL, an $8 billion development project created a new federal administrative capital, Putrajaya, in 1995. KL remains the legislative (lawmaking) capital. The entire transfer of government offices to Putrajaya will not be complete until 2010, when the city is expected to hold 300,000 people.

IPOH (population 566,000), Malaysia's second-largest city, is a center for tin mining. Founded by Chinese miners, it lies on West Malaysia's heavily populated western side. This city is named after the ipoh tree. Malay people once used sap from the ipoh tree as poison on their hunting darts.

OTHER CITIES Johor Baharu (385,000), known as JB, is the capital of the state of Johor, the peninsula's southernmost and most populous state. The region is a center for agriculture. JB is connected to Singapore by a 3,405 foot-long (1,038 m) causeway and by rail.

Melaka (370,000) is a historic port city on the peninsula's west coast. Its Chinese, Islamic, and European heritage is evident in its architecture, cuisine, and culture. Tourism is one of the city's prime industries.

A port on the South China Sea, Kota Kinabalu (population 354,000) is the capital of Sabah. It was completely rebuilt after fighting during World War II destroyed it. The peak of Mount Kinabalu is visible in the distance.

George Town (population 220,000) is a trading center on beauti-

Christ Church *(right)* is a fine example of Dutch architecture in Melaka. The Dutch started to build this church in 1741. It was completed in 1753.

ful Penang Island, one of Malaysia's most visited spots. The British established a naval base here in 1786. The city has encouraged trade over the years by becoming a free port (where goods shipped in and out of the country are not taxed).

A center of trade and the state capital of Sarawak, Kuching (population 152,000) lies 10 miles (16 km) inland from the coast. The Sarawak River divides the city into residential and commercial districts. *Kuching* means "cat" in Malay, and the city hosts a cat museum.

HISTORY AND GOVERNMENT

Archaeological finds at the Niah Caves in Sarawak show that humans inhabited the Malaysian region as long as 50,000 years ago. Archaeologists think that the earliest people in Malaysia lived in caves and hunted wild animals. This early Stone Age population remained undisturbed in the forests of Malaysia until about 2000 B.C. Late Stone Age people, who had more complex stone tools, then moved into Malaysia, probably from southwestern China. The newcomers, known as Proto-Malays (*proto* means "first"), were the ancestors of modern-day Malays. Another wave of immigrants arrived in Malaysia about 250 B.C., bringing knowledge of how to make metal tools.

⊙ Early Influences

Since prehistoric times, the two giants of the Asian continent—India and China—have influenced Southeast Asia. Indian and Chinese merchants traveled to the shores of Malaysia in search of gold, spices, and other valuable goods.

Beginning in the second century A.D., Indian merchants developed trading centers along the western coast of the peninsula. The Malay people began to absorb India's cultural heritage, including Hinduism (the dominant religion of India since about 1500 B.C.). Over the next centuries, different parts of the Malay Peninsula were controlled by various Southeast Asian kingdoms. In the sixth century, China began to demand tribute (payments) and trade from the small empires in the region.

At the beginning of the seventh century, the powerful empire of Sri Vijaya from the island of Sumatra (modern-day Indonesia) extended its influence over the Malay Peninsula. This empire brought Buddhism (a religious faith that originated in India during the fifth century B.C.) to the Malay Peninsula. However, other regional powers later sought to control Sri Vijayan holdings. Rival empires attacked the Sri Vijaya Empire as early as A.D. 992. But the empire long remained the dominant force on the peninsula.

By the end of the twelfth century, some Chinese merchants moved permanently to West Malaysia. Their settlements became the foundation for the future growth of Chinese commercial power in Malaysia. In the thirteenth century, the Sri Vijaya Empire fell to the Majapahit Empire of Java (part of modern Indonesia).

Chinese traders also gradually established a presence on Borneo. By the fourteenth century, the Chinese had become so involved on the island that Chinese names for places became prominent.

The Rise of Melaka and the Arrival of Islam

At the beginning of the fifteenth century, Paramesvara, a refugee prince from Sumatra, murdered the ruler of Tumasik (present-day Singapore) and seized control of the area. Paramesvara made his way up the Malay Peninsula to the western coastal village of Melaka. This small settlement was on a key shipping route across from Sumatra. In 1403 Paramesvara established his rule at Melaka and soon built the city into a thriving and powerful port city. China supported the trading empire that emerged under Paramesvara. Melakan rulers after Paramesvara expanded trade throughout the region, and the realm grew to include a large portion of the peninsula.

Meanwhile, the religion of Islam arrived in Melaka. Islam emerged in the seventh-century Arabian Peninsula through the prophet (spiritual spokesperson) Muhammad. In 1445 Muzaffar Shah, a local Malay leader, became ruler of Melaka and made Islam the territory's official religion. Muzaffar Shah, taking the title of sultan (an Islamic title of nobility), set in motion a rapid spread of Islam to other parts of Southeast Asia. Most Malays eventually became Muslims (followers of Islam). The religion gained a strong foothold on Borneo, and in the late fifteenth century, the Islamic kingdom of Brunei was established on the northern coast.

The rulers of Melaka long recognized the importance of trade. In 1468 Sultan Shah said, "We have learned that to master the blue oceans people must engage in commerce and trade. . . . life has never been so affluent in previous generations as it is today." Visit www.vgsbooks.com for links to more information about the history and government of Malaysia.

European Interest

Melaka's success eventually attracted European explorers who had begun to sail across the Indian Ocean in search of spices and wealth. In

The Strait of Malacca may be seen through a window in a **wall of Santiago Gate** (Porta de Santiago), which still stands in Melaka. The Portuguese built the structure in the early 1500s.

Spices from Asia such as cinnamon and pepper were in heavy demand in Europe as flavorings and preservatives in an age before refrigeration. A successful trading voyage could bring European merchants a profit that was at least four times as high as the cost of the entire expedition.

1511 a well-armed Portuguese fleet captured Melaka from the Malays after intense fighting. But because the Portuguese were primarily interested in trade, they did not establish a colonial government to rule the local population.

The Portuguese introduced Asian spices to Europeans. Opportunities for quick profits from the spice trade soon attracted British and Dutch traders. To organize commercial activity in Indian and Asian waters, British traders established the British East India Company (BEIC) in 1600, and the Dutch began the United East India Company in 1602.

In the following decades, Portugal's hold on lands in Southeast Asia weakened as the Dutch increased their activity in the area. The Dutch also made a few contacts in Borneo beginning in the seventeenth century. In 1641 the Dutch seized Melaka from the Portuguese. The city soon declined in importance, however, because the main Dutch port on the island of Java took away much of Melaka's trade. Although Melaka had been prosperous under the sultans and the Portuguese, most Malays gained little from the rich trading center.

The British were the next Europeans to gain power in Malaya, as the region came to be known under British rule. The British East India Company signed an agreement with one of the sultans of the region in 1786. The document allowed the British to settle on Penang Island and to establish a naval station (modern-day George Town) and trading facilities. In return, the sultan asked for an annual payment and for British protection.

In 1819 Stamford Raffles from the BEIC selected the island of Singapore at the very tip of the peninsula as the site for a new trading center. At first a desolate and almost unpopulated island, Singapore became a major seaport under Raffles's guidance.

In 1824 the Dutch gave up their Malaysian holdings to the British. In 1826 the BEIC combined Melaka and the islands of Penang and Singapore into a single territory known as the Straits Settlements. The company managed the settlement's trade from its headquarters in India.

SKULL TROPHIES

For centuries, many Dayaks, the original inhabitants of Borneo, were headhunters. Warfare among Dayak groups was common, and it was considered a sign of strength for a young man to seek out and cut off a rival warrior's head. According to Dayak belief, the head contains the soul, skill, and strength of the person, even after death. People treated these skull trophies with great care and respect. They removed the brains and then dried the heads over a fire. The dried heads were kept in head houses next to the community's dwellings. Food and ritual offerings were placed in the head houses to persuade the spirits to give aid. Dayaks believed that the spirits had power to protect against enemies, to bring rain, and to increase rice harvests.

○ Borneo

At the time that the British rose in power on and around the peninsula, the thick and steamy rain forests of Borneo remained largely unexplored by Europeans. The indigenous people of Borneo are collectively referred to as the Dayak, meaning "person of the interior." Most Dayaks were hunter-gatherers and rice farmers. Each group, such as the largest, the Iban, had its own separate language and culture. Different groups often engaged in struggles with one another over land and other conflicts.

Most of the northern coast of Borneo was under the sultan of Brunei's leadership. Various chiefs of the Iban and other Dayak groups constantly threatened the sultan's control over the territory. When the British adventurer James Brooke arrived in Borneo in 1839 with armed ships, the sultan's kingdom was in the middle of a rebellion. The sultan of Brunei

The **skulls of enemies whom Dayak warriors killed** became part of the Dayaks' spiritual practices.

accepted Brooke's offer of aid, and the rebellion was quickly put down. In 1841 the sultan granted Brooke the title of raja (prince) of the western section of present-day Sarawak. Brooke established his capital at Kuching and began ruling his private kingdom. He paid the sultan a small annual tribute in return.

The Brooke family became known as the white rajas. Under the rule of this British family, the Dayak leaders agreed to stop headhunting and to settle disputes peacefully. When James Brooke died, his nephew, Charles Brooke, inherited control of Sarawak. The territory grew as the new raja purchased land, and soon the sultan of Brunei was left with only two small pieces of territory.

Discovery of Tin and Growth of British Rule

Large deposits of tin ore were discovered on the western side of the peninsula in the second half of the 1800s. Chinese financiers in the Straits Settlements supplied the capital (the original investment of money) to develop tin mines and to bring thousands of workers from China. The mine owners often treated the Chinese immigrants badly, and many of the workers died from disease.

In 1857 the British government began to administer the Straits Settlements directly instead of from India. In 1867—after years of prompting by merchants of Singapore, Penang, and Melaka—the British declared the Straits Settlements to be a colony. The British encouraged ethnic divisions in the colony. British colonists generally did not mingle socially with Malaysians. An elite group of Malays gained British-style educations and served in government jobs. Most Malays continued to farm and fish in their kampongs. The Chinese were merchants and tin miners.

The Chinese mine workers organized into competitive secret societies and frequently fought one another. The local Malay rulers added to the tense situation by quarreling over their share of the tax money from the Chinese-owned tin mines. Demands for a solution to these difficulties came from both British and Chinese commercial leaders of the Straits Settlements. These leaders viewed the bloodshed, violence, and pirate raids along the coasts as bad for business.

British rule on the peninsula outside the Straits Settlement was indirect. The British established a system of resident advisers to control the local Malay rulers. In 1874 the British governor of the Straits Settlements and Sultan Abdullah, the strongest local leader, signed the Treaty of Pangkor. The treaty made the British the real rulers of the region, and the sultan's role became mainly ceremonial.

During colonial times, China was a major source of foreign workers in Malaysia. Some of these Chinese became wealthy and powerful. Between 1868 and 1885, Yap Ah Loy was the Kapitan China, or leader of the Chinese, in Kuala Lumpur. He owned one out of every three buildings in town and ran many of them as brothels (houses of prostitution). He also held large tin-mining and plantation interests. Meanwhile, most Chinese workers lived in conditions similar to slavery.

The territory of present-day Sabah was much sought after by European traders, who called it North Borneo. European merchants, seeking the precious hardwoods of the rain forest, made many attempts to sign timber-cutting agreements. In 1881 trading rights finally went to the British North Borneo Company. This British business administered Sabah for the British government.

Other regions of the peninsula also accepted resident officials. Four centrally located territories, including Perak, merged into the Federated Malay States in

British travel writer **Isabella L. Bird** *(right)* **toured Perak** from the back of an Asian elephant in 1879 and later published a book about her adventure.

1896. A treaty between Great Britain and Thailand in 1909 brought the northern peninsular states under British control. In 1913 the entire peninsula and northwestern Borneo were loosely united in a federation called British Malaya. Through family rule, direct colonial rule, and the indirect rule of resident advisers and businesses, the British controlled all of modern-day Malaysia.

Rubber and Prosperity

A major event in the world's economy in the early years of the twentieth century was a rubber boom, fueled by the new demand for automobile tires. Rubber tree plantations eventually covered 7,500 square miles (19,425 sq. km) of land in West Malaysia. Thousands of workers emigrated from India to work on the rubber plantations, and rubber soon surpassed tin as Malaysia's leading export.

Compared to the rest of Southeast Asia, the peninsula was a prosperous and stable place under British rule during the first four decades of the twentieth century. It provided 60 percent of the world's tin and 40 percent of the world's rubber. With great wealth and a relatively small population, the peninsular states could provide roads, railways, mosquito control, and telephone lines—all of which were rare services in Southeast Asia.

By 1931 the Chinese population of British Malaya numbered 1.7 million, and the native Malay population numbered only 1.6 million. Some Chinese who lived in West Malaysia grew wealthy. Indian laborers also earned more money on the peninsula than they did in India. The Malays generally did not fare as well economically as foreign workers did. Despite their advantages working in colonial government jobs, Malays controlled very few of their country's economic resources. The Chinese owned most shops, factories, mines, and other businesses.

Some Malaysians, especially a number of Chinese, were discontented with British rule and became Communist activists. They worked to establish a system of communal, public ownership of the land and the means of production (businesses and factories). Assisted by organizers from China, the Communists led labor strikes in the 1930s. Meanwhile, Malay Muslim fundamentalists, who believed in a strict interpretation of Islamic religious law, preached that the British-style system of government was incompatible with Islam.

Despite these agitations, satisfaction among most Malaysians from all ethnic groups created a conservative political climate. Unlike in other Southeast Asian colonies, no significant movement for self-rule emerged in British Malaya. Then, on December 8, 1941—one day after the Japanese attack on the U.S. naval base at Pearl Harbor—the Japanese invasion of the peninsula began. World War II had come to Malaysia.

▶ The Japanese Occupation and Postwar Malaysia

The Japanese quickly defeated the British in battles throughout the Malay Peninsula and overtook Borneo with little resistance. After their occupation in early 1942, the Japanese ruled from Singapore, imprisoning Europeans and appointing Malays to many administrative posts.

Several anti-Japanese resistance groups arose in response to the occupation. The most important groups were the well organized, mostly Chinese Communist guerrilla fighters and the Malayan People's Anti-Japanese Army. Chinese Malaysians strongly opposed the Japanese, who had invaded China in the 1930s. The Japanese occupiers brutally persecuted the Chinese, and thousands of Chinese were executed or "disappeared" in Malaysia. Many of their bodies were found in mass graves after the war. Guerrilla resistance to the Japanese continued throughout the war, all over the region. For instance, the Kelabit indigenous people of Borneo, armed mostly with traditional blowpipes, paired with an Australian force to win several victories

An ethnic Chinese Malaysian soldier watches the Singapore harbor for signs of a Japanese air raid. The British had expected the Japanese army to arrive by sea. But the Japanese landed in northeast Malaysia and quickly moved troops down the peninsula—on bicycles.

over the Japanese. In 1945 U.S. forces and their allies defeated Japan, and World War II ended.

After the war, the Brooke family gave Sarawak, the family's private kingdom for more than one hundred years, to Great Britain as a colony. When the British returned to power in Malaysia, they faced many challenges in ruling a divided country. Malays and Chinese distrusted each other because of their different treatment by the Japanese during the war. The British proposed a Malayan Union with equal citizenship for all, under British rule. Malays feared Chinese majority power in such a union. They formed the United Malays National Organization (UMNO) to fight against the plan. The Malays wanted to be a majority in whatever nation emerged after the war.

As a compromise, in February 1948, the British established the Federation of Malaya. The federation (loose political union) kept local power in the hands of the Malay sultans and limited non-Malay citizenship. Malays had become a united political group by working together to reject the first British proposal. But the second governmental plan caused great ethnic-based hostility between Malays and non-Malays.

The Emergency and Independence

After the federation, the Chinese Communists who had fought against the Japanese occupation began an uprising against British rule. On June 16, 1948, Communist guerrillas entered two rubber estates near Ipoh and killed four British planters. The incident set off a period known as the Emergency. Guerrilla tactics and a frightened population made the Communists a powerful opponent for government troops. But the Communists' civilian supporters—who supplied the fighters with food and other essentials—were few in number. Many Malays did not want British rule, but they did not want to join forces with the Chinese either. In addition, calls for independence did not seem necessary because the British—greatly weakened by World War II—had already begun the process of granting Malaya self-rule.

When it became apparent in the mid-1950s that the Communists had little hope of taking over, Great Britain urged the region to become a fully independent nation. The main political leader in the peninsula at that time was Tunku Abdul Rahman. His party, UMNO, had joined with the Malayan Chinese and Indian parties to create the Alliance Party. This multiethnic party won many seats in 1955 during the elections for Malaya's first legislature. Finally, on August 31, 1957, the Federation of Malaya achieved *merdeka* (independence), and Rahman became the new nation's first prime minister.

Tunku Abdul Rahman *(seated center)* prepares to sign the agreement that will create the independent Federation of Malaya, effective August 31, 1957. Rahman became the new nation's first prime minister.

At independence, Malays controlled government and agriculture but owned only 2.5 percent of the nation's businesses. Chinese business interests owned over 30 percent, while foreigners, mainly British, owned the rest. In framing the constitution, leaders of the major ethnic groups—Malays, Chinese, and Indians—agreed to citizenship for all and a system of special privileges for Malays. To help boost Malay economic development, the 1957 constitution gave Malays preference for some education, loans, business permits, and government jobs. They hoped this system would create better relations between ethnic groups by removing inequalities.

The Emergency ended officially in 1960. The attempted Communist takeover failed in part because, unlike in some other Southeast Asian countries such as Vietnam, few Malaysians were discontented enough to join the campaign.

In the early years of independence, Malaysians debated about where to draw the boundaries of the new nation. At first, the federation included only the eleven states of West Malaysia. Singapore was a separate British colony but wanted to merge with Malaysia. Most Malays opposed such a union because Singapore's largely Chinese population would make the Malays a minority in the federation.

After much debate, Singapore, Sarawak, and Sabah voted to join the new nation. These states became part of the newly named independent Federation of Malaysia on September 16, 1963. The additions assured that the number of Dayaks would keep the Chinese from becoming the majority. These Bornean ethnic groups received the same special privileges that Malays enjoyed. The result was that Malaysian society was split into bumiputras who receive special privileges, and nonbumiputras, who do not. Bumiputras are Malaysians who belong to ethnic groups that predate the arrival of Indian, Chinese, or European immigrants.

Ethnic Relations and the 1969 Riots

In the 1960s, conflicts arose between bumiputras and nonbumiputras over the system of privileges. Singapore leader Lee Kuan Yew pushed for what he called a Malaysian Malaysia, in which all citizens would have equal rights. But Malays feared that without their special privileges, most of the economic power in the federation would remain in Chinese hands. On August 9, 1965, Singapore withdrew from the Federation of Malaysia and became an independent nation.

By 1969 many nonbumiputras had become very resentful of the privilege system. Much of this resentment focused on their political leaders in the Alliance Party who had given away nonbumiputra rights. In the

Rioting ethnic Malays and ethnic Chinese wrecked and burned homes in Kuala Lumpur during a week of violence in 1969. Residents saved what they could.

elections for parliament (the lawmaking body) held on May 10, 1969, the Alliance lost many seats. Large crowds of Chinese marched in the streets of Kuala Lumpur in celebration of their electoral victory. Street fighting between the Chinese, the Indians, and the Malays broke out in KL. When the riots were over, hundreds of Malaysians—mostly Chinese and Indians—had been killed.

The ethnic riots shocked Malaysians from every ethnic group. Tunku Abdul Rahman, whom the Malays saw as too sympathetic to the concerns of nonbumiputras, resigned in 1970. Tun Abdul Razak replaced him as prime minister. The ruling council then outlawed debate over bumiputra privileges. To promote Malay culture, they also made the Malay language, Bahasa Malaysia, the official language of government.

The Visions of Mahathir

The next year, a broad group of political parties, known as the Barisan Nasional (BN, or National Front), came to power. The BN was made up of the original core of the Alliance, but many smaller parties joined as well, including the Parti Islam Se-Malaysia (PAS). This Muslim fundamentalist group wanted the Malaysian government to be entirely Islamic. This issue was another dividing point between Malaysia's ethnic groups, since Malays are Muslim while most non-Malays are not.

In 1971 the government introduced the New Economic Policy (NEP) to create a better balance of economic power among the nation's ethnic groups. Dr. Mahathir Mohamed, an outspoken UMNO leader and a physician by training, was the main designer of the policy. Its most ambitious goal was to give bumiputras eventual control over 30 percent of Malaysia's economic resources. A quota system guaranteed Malay representation in government, business, and education.

The NEP improved the lives of many bumiputras, and Mahathir became Malaysia's prime minister in 1981. Mahathir proved to be a powerful, outspoken, and sometimes controversial leader. His vision was to transform Malaysia into a modern, industrialized Asian nation. His plans included diversifying the country's economy from rubber and tin production into manufacturing. This met with great success, and Malaysia became the world's eighth-fastest growing economy in the 1980s.

However, Mahathir also held power by suppressing civil rights. The Internal Security Act (ISA)—originally meant to counter Communist terrorism during the Emergency—allows the government to arrest people and hold them without trial. In October 1987, Mahathir claimed that ethnic clashes were threatening to become violent. So, using the ISA, he ordered the arrest of more than one hundred of his political opponents. He also closed three major newspapers and banned all public gatherings. Although these moves drew international criticism, Mahathir said that such authoritarian methods against opponents to his rule were necessary. He silenced dissent even further by passing a harsh censorship law.

Leaders of Western (European and North American) countries often criticized Mahathir, who frequently made anti-Western comments. He strongly objected to Western interference in developing Asian countries. He worked to build bonds between Asian countries so they could help one another and not have to rely on aid from Western countries.

Malaysia's economic success meant that Mahathir mostly remained a popular leader at home. The prosperity benefited all ethnic groups and reduced tension between them. In 1992 Mahathir outlined an ambitious plan that became known as Vision 2020. The plan called for Malaysia to be a fully developed, industrialized country by the year 2020, with an average income per person that matches the earnings of Western nations. It also called for ethnic harmony in a united Malaysian nation and the growth of a mature democratic society. Many challenges stood in the way.

● The "Greening" of Malaysia

One of the challenges to Malaysia's unity was the revival of Islamic fundamentalism, or the drive to make Islam the dominant political, legal, and social force. Mahathir (a Muslim, like most Malays) and his government opposed extreme fundamentalist demands that would threaten the harmony of the multiethnic nation. In the early 1990s, for example, the government avoided passing laws that would have made all Malaysians, both Muslim and non-Muslim, subject to Islamic law (called Sharia). Some fundamentalist Islamic groups also pushed for outlawing all alcohol and gambling and for enforcing conservative clothing styles in all of Malaysia. Non-Muslim Chinese and Indians and many Muslim bumiputras did not want such legal restrictions.

Most fundamentalists work through political means. But Malaysia also saw a rise in militant Islam, or Muslim groups willing to use violence to achieve their ends. Not only did such militants pose a security risk to the nation but they also potentially scared away international investors. The government acted in various ways to undermine militant influences. For instance, in the summer of 1994, the government banned al-Arqam, an Islamic sect that operated businesses and more than two hundred schools in Malaysia, claiming it preached militant Islam.

The administration did encourage an increase of voluntary Islamic practices in Malaysian society, such as head scarves for women and daily prayer. Green is the color of Islam, and the term "the greening of Malaysia" refers to this gradual Islamization. This increase, along with Mahathir's support, helped Anwar Ibrahim, a Muslim fundamentalist leader, to rise in the ranks of the government. Anwar eventually was named deputy prime minister. Many observers felt that he was the likely successor to Mahathir.

Rising and Falling

In the mid-1990s, Mahathir proposed a revision in the laws that would lessen discrimination against the country's Indian and Chinese citizens. The measure proved widely popular and helped BN win a sweeping victory in elections held in April 1995.

Malaysia's economy continued to perform extremely well under Mahathir's guidance. The economy had successfully developed from one based on natural products to one based on manufacturing, especially the manufacturing and export of electrical goods and appliances. The government next developed plans for Malaysia to expand into high-tech products, including computer software. Kuala Lumpur's Petronas Towers—headquarters of PETRONAS, the country's oil industry management agency—became the world's tallest buildings when construction began in the mid-1990s. Rising eighty-eight floors, they were a symbol of Malaysia's steady advance toward full industrial development.

This advance came to a halt in 1997, when an economic crisis swept through Southeast Asia. Malaysia's stock market and currency lost almost half their value. Mahathir implemented his own economic plans in response, and Malaysia's ailing economy improved more quickly than that of other Southeast Asian countries. But growth remained slow afterward.

Mahathir's deputy prime minister Anwar Ibrahim disagreed with Mahathir's handling of the crisis. In a controversial move, Mahathir had Anwar arrested under the Internal Security Act. Anwar faced charges of corrupt conduct. Many observers worldwide believed the charges were false and politically motivated. Demonstrators took to the streets of Kuala Lumpur, but Anwar was sentenced to fifteen years in prison.

The Twenty-First Century

Mahathir's sometimes tense relations with Western leaders improved after terrorists struck the United States on September 11, 2001. The terrorists had links to al-Qaeda, a militant Islamic network. Two of the terrorists also had ties to a Malaysian former army captain. Mahathir, who had long spoken about the dangers of militant Islam, pledged to continue to oppose it at home and around the world. Malaysia became an ally of the United States in the fight against global terrorism. The two countries established an antiterrorism training center in Malaysia.

The Malaysian government claimed that migrants working illegally in the country posed a security risk. About 1 million workers, mostly from Malaysia's poorer neighbor Indonesia, do many of Malaysia's unwanted dirty or dangerous jobs. Many do not have proper legal papers to be in the country. In 2002, new laws against illegal immigrants came into effect. The tough laws carry sentences of whipping, fines, and prison terms for offenders. A mass departure of 300,000 people followed. Most of them were from Indonesia and ended up in refugee camps there.

In October 2003, Mahathir resigned after twenty-two years as prime minister. Abdullah Badawi, an Islamic scholar and a close associate of Mahathir, became prime minister. His party, Barisan Nasional, won a landslide victory in the March 2004 elections. Soon afterward, Malaysia's Federal Court overturned Anwar's conviction, and he was released in September 2004.

In December 2004, Malaysia was mostly spared when a tsunami, or massive ocean wave, hit parts of Southeast Asia. Indonesia took the

"CIVILIZATION ISLAM"

In 2005 Prime Minister Abdullah declared of Malaysia, "We are a very moderate Islamic country." Unlike in conservative Muslim countries such as Saudi Arabia, in Malaysia men and women freely socialize, eat, and dress as they please. Abdullah promotes what he calls Islam Hadhari, or Civilization Islam. This vision stresses the value of tolerance, the development of education and economic opportunities, and the use of persuasion in religion, not force. However, some Muslims point out that Malaysia does not give its Muslim citizens full civil rights. Only Muslims are subject to the Islamic justice system that governs personal law. The Islamic police are allowed to arrest Muslims for acts such as drinking alcohol or gambling, while non-Muslims go free. Many Muslims also object to laws in some states that deny Muslim women equal rights with men. And as long as Muslims aren't allowed to adopt another religion, critics say, Malaysians do not have freedom of religion.

brunt of the waves' destruction, with deaths in the tens of thousands. Because of the tsunami, the Malaysian government put off another deportation of Indonesian illegal immigrants. But in spring 2005, a roundup of illegal immigrants saw the forced departure of hundreds of thousands of workers.

Although Malaysia has made great strides, Vision 2020 is far from being realized. The country's gross national income (GNI) of about $9,000 per person is higher than the average GNI of about $4,000 per person in other less developed countries. But it is still less than the $24,000 GNI average per person in more developed countries. Ethnic discrimination is legal, and the government can imprison people without trial. But despite the challenges Malaysia faces, the nation is an economic success with ambitious plans to further develop its high-technology sector. Malaysians of all religions continue to hotly debate the proper place of Islam in the political life of their country, but ethnic relations remain peaceful in this multicultural country.

Governmental Structure

Since independence in 1957, Malaysia's government runs on a federal parliamentary system. The federal government is the central authority in national matters. The parliament is the branch of government that makes laws. The prime minister, who is a member of parliament, holds executive power. The system allows each of the thirteen states to retain authority over some local affairs. All citizens aged twenty-one and older have voting rights.

Malaysia is a constitutional monarchy, which means its ruler has inherited power that is limited by a constitution. Although nine of the Malaysian states have ruling monarchs—called sultans—no nationwide monarchy existed when the federation began. The constitution therefore established that every five years the sultans would meet to choose one from among the nine rulers to reign as *yang di-pertuan agong* (supreme ruler) of Malaysia until their next meeting. The role of this temporary monarch, customarily referred to as the king, is mostly ceremonial. The king is also the leader of the country's Islamic faith.

A sultan—or a governor in those states that have no sultan—is the head of each state and wields political influence. Most power rests with the state's elected legislative assembly. At the federal level, power resides in parliament and in the cabinet of advisers led by the prime minister.

The national parliament consists of two houses, the House of Representatives (Dewan Rakyat) and the Senate (Dewan Negara). The 219 members of the Dewan Rakyat are elected directly by the people of Malaysia and do most of the legislative work. The 70 members of the

Dewan Negara are appointed—some by the state legislatures and some by the king—and function as advisers and honorary representatives.

The prime minister is the most powerful person in the Malaysian government. Whoever is the president of the majority political party in the Dewan Rakyat automatically becomes the prime minister.

Malaysia's legal system is based on British common law. The prime minister advises the king in making appointments to the ten-member Federal Court, Malaysia's highest judicial body. The Federal Court hears appeals from two high courts, one in West Malaysia and the other alternating between Sabah and Sarawak. A lower-court judge and jury try capital cases (for which the punishment may be execution) and kidnappings. Sharia courts hear cases on certain matters that pertain only to Muslims, such as Islamic rulings on moral behavior.

THE PEOPLE

With a population of almost 26 million people, Malaysia's population density—201 people per square mile (77 per square km)—is far lower than the Southeast Asian average of 316 people per sq. mile (122 per sq. km). About 62 percent of Malaysia's population lives in urban areas. The average Malaysian woman has 3.3 children in her lifetime. Malaysia's population includes a large percentage of young people—34 percent is under the age of 15. As young women reach childbearing age, the country's population will keep growing. It is expected to reach 47 million by 2050.

For a small country, Malaysia has a wide diversity of peoples living within its boundaries. The nation's largest ethnic groups are bumiputras, with Malays making up 51 percent. Bumiputras also include other indigenous peoples, who make up 11 percent. Chinese people (24 percent) and Indians (8 percent) make up the largest nonbumiputra groups. People of European or other descent compose another 6 percent. These different groups have developed side-by-side cultures and celebrate their own holidays, speak their own languages, and even pursue separate traditional jobs.

The special benefits that bumiputras receive divide them from the other ethnic groups. Nevertheless, the government has tried to promote a shared national identity. For example, laws have declared certain ethnic holidays to be national holidays for all. These include Chinese New Year, Indian Diwali (the Hindu Festival of Lights), and Malay Hari Raya Puasa (celebrated at the end of the Muslim holy month of Ramadan). Such celebrations include open houses, encourage social mixing, and provide occasions for goodwill among the ethnic groups.

Majority Ethnic Groups

Malay bumiputras control most of Malaysia's government. The NEP of the 1970s and 1980s reserved a number of government jobs for Malays. The policy encouraged more Malays to move to the cities, where they could take a bigger part in Malaysia's economic life. Modern Malays have become involved in the economic sectors of their nation. Yet in the twenty-first century, Malays own only 23 percent of

Malaysia's assets. Many Malays live in a traditional manner in kampongs near rivers or streams. The major occupations of these Malays are farming rice fields, working on small rubber plantations, and fishing in the rivers or along the coasts. Many Malays make their homes along West Malaysia's eastern coast—in the states of Kelantan and Terengganu—and in the northern states of Kedah and Perlis. A significant Malay middle class has emerged, and some Malays have become extremely wealthy through taking advantage of government contracts. Almost all Malays are Muslims.

For links to more information about Malaysia's ethnic and religious diversity and for up-to-date demographics for the Malaysian population, go to www.vgsbooks.com.

Chinese Malaysians are often businesspeople and shopkeepers, and they hold many important positions in commerce and industry. Most Chinese Malaysians are descendants of the large wave of immigrants who came from China in the late nineteenth and early twentieth centuries, when tin mining became a major industry. At the center of Chinese life is the extended family. The family forms the basis of the business community, and supplies, credit, and employment opportunities are distributed among family members. Honoring ancestors is an important Chinese value. Most Chinese are Buddhists or follow other traditional Asian faiths.

The majority of Malaysia's Indian community comes from the southeastern Indian state of Tamil Nadu. For statistical purposes, the Malaysian government also considers people with ancestors from Pakistan, Bangladesh, or Sri Lanka to be Indians. A demand for laborers on rubber estates during the early twentieth century brought many Indian immigrants to Malaysia. One of the main reasons the Indians willingly came to Malaya was because of the caste, or class, system in India. Under this practice, those who are born into the lower castes can never improve their standing in society. In Malaysia Indians could improve their status. The Indians who came to Malaysia brought along their Hindu culture with its ornate temples, flavorful cuisine, and colorful clothing. Hindu traditions remain strong in Malaysia's Indian community. Indians have become active in trade and commerce, and they make up a large share of the construction force on the Malaysian railways, buildings, roads, and bridges. Other Indian Malaysians work in the nation's banking and investment industries.

Other Ethnic Groups

Besides Malays, bumiputras include many other groups. In West Malaysia, these peoples are generally known as the Orang Asli (original people), but they are not a unified ethnic community. Most of the Orang Asli live a traditional life as hunters and gatherers in the deep forests of the peninsula. Many of them supplement their livelihoods with small-scale agriculture—such as planting rice—but large permanent settlements are not part of the Orang Asli way of life. Government efforts to extend health care, education, and other social services to the Orang Asli have encouraged some of them to break with tradition and to settle in permanent villages. Deforestation has also displaced many groups. The loss of the rain forest threatens their traditional way of life.

On the island of Borneo, several dozen original ethnic groups, the Dayaks, populate the mountains. The most numerous of the Dayaks are the Iban. They make up about 30 percent of the population of Sarawak. Deforestation has displaced many Iban, and many have taken jobs with the oil companies that operate in eastern Sarawak. Some have moved to Kuching, Bintalu, and other cities. The major Dayak group in Sabah is the Kadazan, composing about 25 percent of the population. In modern times, some of them, too, have moved to cities.

Most Iban, however, still live in the untamed interior of the island. Their large communal dwellings (called longhouses) are raised off the forest floor on stilts. Longhouses shelter about twenty families. The Iban, like most of the other Dayak peoples, plant rice, gather forest vegetables, and raise chickens and pigs. To earn cash for the articles

In a traditional longhouse, **Iban women of Sarawak** display crafts to sell to visitors.

they cannot produce themselves, such as medicine, the Iban grow pepper and cassavas (starchy, edible roots).

People with mixed European and Malaysian or European and other Southeast Asian ancestry are referred to as Eurasians. Malaysian culture has tended to look down on Eurasians. Almost 1 million migrant laborers also live in Malaysia performing the lowest paying and most dangerous jobs. Most of these workers come from Indonesia, which has a high unemployment rate. Many of them are in Malaysia illegally and risk being arrested and deported at any time.

Language

The official language of Malaysia is Bahasa Malaysia, which means "language of Malaysia" and is also called Malay. It belongs to the Malayo-Polynesian family of languages and is related to many tongues of the South Pacific. Bahasa Malaysia and Bahasa Indonesia, the official language of Indonesia, are different dialects of Malay, and speakers of one can easily understand speakers of the other. Malay includes many words from Sanskrit (an ancient Indian language), Arabic (the original language of Islam), and English. At the time of independence, many non-Malays objected to making Malay the nation's official language. They believed that English would be a better compromise. The government, however, decided to choose a language that was not a reminder of its colonial past and was easy to learn. But the government promotes English for practical reasons and international commerce.

Peranakans, which means "half caste" in Malay, are people of mixed Chinese and Malay ancestry. Their ancestors were often wealthy merchants in the 1500s and onwards who used the name and religion of their Chinese fathers but kept the Malay traditions of their mothers. Chinese and Malay languages blended into a distinct Peranakan dialect, which also includes some European influences. Peranakans are often called Straits Chinese or Baba-Nonyas, from the Peranakan words for "males" (baba) and "females" (nonya).

The use of the official language is not universal in Malaysia. The Dayak peoples of the Sarawak and Sabah forests have little contact with speakers of Bahasa Malaysia. They mostly speak their traditional languages of Iban, Kadazan, or various others. Chinese dialects spoken in Malaysia are Cantonese, Mandarin, Hokkien, and Hakka. Indians speak Tamil and other Indian languages.

English, the official language used during the colonial period, is widely spoken in Malaysia, and a number of urban Malaysians of Chinese or Indian descent speak it as their primary language. Besides learning English as a subject in school, Malaysians have a great deal of exposure to the language from U.S., British, and Australian programs that regularly appear on Malaysian television.

Education

Children in Malaysia begin primary school at the age of six, and education is free through secondary school. Bahasa Malaysia, Chinese, or Tamil are the languages of instruction, depending on the language of the students. In 2003 English was reintroduced as a language of instruction. English and Bahasa Malaysia are taught as subjects in all schools, whatever the primary language of instruction.

After six years of primary school, students attend secondary school for three years. Each year of secondary school is called a form. Students progress through the forms by passing tests in areas such as art, science, technical topics, or vocational subjects. They choose which areas to specialize in during the upper forms.

MALAY GREETINGS

Like English, Malay uses the Roman alphabet. Here is a sampling of Malay greetings with English translations:

MALAY	ENGLISH
Salamat pagi	Good morning.
Salamat tengah-hari	Good afternoon
Salamat malam	Good night
Salamat tinggal	Good-bye

Muslim Malay schoolgirls in Kuala Terengganu pose for a photo in front of a mural of traditional boats. Their region is famous for boat making.

Malaysia has many technical colleges, teacher training colleges, and national universities. Three universities give master's degrees and doctorates as well as undergraduate degrees. The oldest and best known is the University of Malaya. Located in Kuala Lumpur, the university includes a medical school and a law school. Public universities give preference to admitting bumiputras. Many nonbumiputras attend private universities or go abroad for college education.

Malaysia has a well-educated society, even though some of its regions are isolated and hard to reach. Almost 100 percent of Malaysian children attend primary school, though this drops to 53 percent for secondary school. About 91 percent of Malaysian men and 84 percent of Malaysian women are literate, or able to read and write.

Health

The quality of health care in Malaysia is very high, due to strong governmental support of programs in health education, nutrition, hygiene, and preventive medicine, including immunization. The infant mortality rate (the number of deaths among babies before their first birthday) is a good indicator of the general health of a country. Malaysia's has declined from 102 deaths per 1,000 live births in 1974 to 11 deaths per 1,000 babies. This is a much lower rate than the region as a whole. Southeast Asia averages 41 infant deaths per 1,000. The maternal death rate (the number of women who die giving birth) is 4 women per every 1,000 births as opposed to 30 for every 1,000 in Southeast Asia. The average life expectancy for Malaysians is 73 years old (71 for males and 76 for females).

Medical personnel and hospital facilities in Malaysia are of high quality, though urban areas generally have better care than rural areas. The government helps pay for medical care, so fees are low and all people can get health care. Government efforts to control disease-carrying mosquitoes have sharply reduced the incidence of malaria, once a major ailment throughout Malaysia. However, diseases caused by contaminated food and water, such as bacterial diarrhea, hepatitis A, cholera, and typhoid fever, are widespread. The human immunodeficiency virus (HIV), the virus that often causes acquired immunodeficiency syndrome (AIDS), affects 0.4 percent of the adult population. The government promotes education to fight the deadly spread of AIDS.

Women

Malaysian secular (nonreligious) law gives men and women equal rights, and women make up 15 percent of the country's parliament, a percentage that is growing. Some Malaysian women are active in politics and occupy top jobs in the business world. For instance, the head of the Bank of Malaysia (the central bank), Zeti Akhtar Aziz, is a woman. Marina

In 2005 **Malay Muslim women participate in a protest against atomic weapons.** The event, a march through downtown Kuala Lumpur, coincides with the sixtieth anniversary of the atomic bombing of Hiroshima, Japan. Some Malaysian women take pride in their involvement in global politics.

Mahathir, the daughter of former prime minister Mahathir, is a well-known activist for human rights, democracy, and AIDS education.

Muslim Malaysian women, however, are subject to Islamic law, which tends to favor men. For instance, Muslim men are allowed to practice polygamy, or have up to four wives, though this is not widely practiced. The Islamic Family Law of 1989 gave Muslim women more legal rights in family matters such as divorce and inheritance. But state laws vary, and in 2002, the state of Perlis passed a law allowing a man to marry a second wife without the first wife's consent.

Some Muslim groups object to interpretations of Islam that deny women full rights. Sisters in Islam is one such Muslim Malaysian group that works for legal rights for women. Islamic law does not restrict Chinese and Indian Malaysian women.

CULTURAL LIFE

In Malaysia, tradition is more than a respect for the past. It is alive in the culture, in religion and ceremonies, and in art and theater. Batik is a method of hand-printing designs on textiles. Batik cloth is an art form that is both useful and full of centuries-old patterns and symbols. Modern artists use batik painting to portray contemporary images. Traditional dances act out age-old tales. Modern architecture draws on traditional forms. The result is a lively and fascinating mix of old and new.

▷ Religion

Religion is very important to Malaysians. Fewer than 1 percent of Malaysians say they belong to no religion. Although Malaysia's constitution guarantees freedom of religion, Islam is the country's official faith and is practiced by 60 percent of Malaysians, including almost all Malays. Although Muslims are free to convert others to Islam, in most of Malaysia it is illegal to attempt to convert a Muslim to another religion. Other faiths Malaysians practice include Buddhism, 19 percent;

Christianity, 9 percent; Hinduism, 6 percent; Confucianism, 3 percent; Taoism, Sikhism, or no religion, 2 percent; and traditional indigenous religions, 1 percent. Syncretism, or the blending of different religious practices and beliefs, occurs too.

Islam

Islam, which means "the will of God" in Arabic, arrived in the country through traders from southern India. This monotheistic (one god) religion shares roots with Jewish and Christian religions. Muslims believe that the prophet Muhammad received messages from Allah (Arabic for "God") through the angel Gabriel. These messages form Islam's holy book, the Quran, written in elegant Arabic.

Five main duties, known as the five pillars of Islam, fall upon Muslims. These are declaring faith in Allah and his prophet; praying five times a day; giving alms (charity) to the poor; fasting during Ramadan; and making a pilgrimage to Mecca (Islam's holiest city, in

Saudi Arabia), if possible. Islam also teaches that people should behave generously, fairly, chastely, honestly, and respectfully.

In addition to the large number of Malay Muslims, a few Indian and Chinese people also follow Islam. Mosques are well attended. Malaysian Muslims often save money for years to pay for the hajj (pilgrimage) to Mecca. Pilgrims who return from the hajj are treated with great respect within the Muslim community and may use the title hajji.

Besides following the Islamic way of life, Muslims in Malaysia also must follow Islamic law. Muslim religious authorities may arrest, fine, physically punish, and jail Muslims for violating Sharia, even if they have broken no civil laws. These laws forbid having sex outside marriage, drinking alcohol, gambling, and more.

Other Faiths

A small number of Chinese are Christians, but most practice Buddhism. This religion teaches a way of liberation from suffering by living a compassionate life, free from desires for worldly things. Buddhism encourages the practice of meditation—a deep mental exercise, like prayer—to increase spiritual awareness. Some Chinese also follow Confucianism or Taoism. Confucianism is more of a social philosophy than a religion. It focuses on practical wisdom and order in family and political life. Taoism leads believers to follow the Tao (the Way) to achieve personal harmony with the universe. Many Chinese also revere their ancestors as part of their religious observance. They make a family shrine out of pictures or belongings of deceased parents or grandparents.

Most of Malaysia's Indians are followers of Hinduism, the world's oldest major religion. The concepts of karma and reincarnation are its central beliefs. Karma is the belief that every action causes a good or bad reaction. Reincarnation is the belief that each being is born over and over again. The karma of previous lives shapes the next lifetime. Eventually, good actions can free the believer from this cycle of death and rebirth. Hindus worship many deities, or gods and goddesses, and build elaborate temples to them. The many deities are representations of different aspects of Brahman, or the Supreme God. The four Veda are the sacred books of Hinduism. The Indian Malaysian population also includes a small percentage of Christians, Muslims, and Sikhs (followers of a religion that developed from Hinduism and Islam).

On Borneo many of the original ethnic groups follow traditional indigenous beliefs. Central to these traditions is the belief that all living and nonliving things have a spirit and that religious activi-

To reach the Batu Caves, visitors must ascend 272 steps.

A HINDU TEMPLE FESTIVAL

The Batu Caves are a network of limestone caves north of Kuala Lumpur. They are the main Hindu pilgrimage site in Malaysia and the location of Thaipusam, one of the most spectacular Hindu celebrations. This event commemorates the day the goddess Parvathi gave her son, Murugan, a *vel* (lance) to destroy three demons threatening the world. A million people visit the Batu Caves every year for the colorful festival of faith, thanksgiving, and hope. Chanting "vel, vel" and accompanied by trance-inducing drums, devotees climb 272 steps to Temple Cave carrying small pots of milk as religious offerings. Hundreds of devotees also attach the pots to their flesh with hooks or pierce their cheeks and tongues with skewers. These devotees prepare for this ordeal by cleansing their bodies and minds with forty days of prayer, fasting, and other devotions. Peacock plumes, ropes of jasmine flowers, and tropical fruits also adorn the caves.

ties can make the spirits friendly to the believers. It is also believed that the spirits of ancestors can go between this world and the next. A large number of the Bornean peoples are Christian and belong mostly to the Anglican (Church of England), Roman Catholic, or Methodist churches.

◉ Literature

The most important historical piece of Malay literature is *Sejarah Melayu (Malay Annals)* from the 1500s. It is a blend of mythical tales and the history of the Malay sultans. In the 1800s, traveler Munshi Abdullah of Melaka wrote about his adventures in Malaysia in *Tales from Abdullah's Travels.*

In the early twentieth century, several famous European authors wrote works based in Malaysia. The hero of Joseph Conrad's classic adventure story *Lord Jim* is based on James Brooke, the white raja of Sarawak. A master of the short story, W. Somerset Maugham captured the flavor of 1920s British colonial life in Malaysia. British novelist Anthony Burgess wrote *The Malayan Trilogy* about the era of Malaysia's drive for independence.

Modern Malaysian authors record the Malaysian experience, often in the English language. Frequently the sensory qualities of the country are the backdrop to the stories—the sound of rain or the smell of tropical flowers, for instance. Themes often involve the personal and political challenges of living in a multicultural society. K. S. Maniam's novel *The Return* (1994) is about an Indian Malaysian returning home after being educated abroad. Shirley Geok-lin Lim's novel *Joss and Gold* (2001) centers on a Chinese Malaysian woman, a teacher of English literature, whose father-in-law is killed in the ethnic riots of 1969. *The Rice Mother* (2003) by Rani Manicka follows the life of a Hindu Malaysian woman. This poetic novel is full of colorful characters such as snake charmers, powerful bankers, and mango merchants. Tash Aw's novel, *The Harmony Silk Factory* (2005), weaves together the fate of a Chinese man and his British friend right before the Japanese invasion of Malaysia.

The poems of two important Malay poets, Allahyarham Usman Awang and Muhammad Haji Salleh, are written in the Malay language. Their work is also available translated into English. Usman, who died in 2001, was Malaysia's National Poet Laureate, or poet of special honor. He was known for his humanism (devotion to human dignity and worth). Muhammad's poetry also values human and natural life. His poem "among vegetables," for instance, celebrates the fragrance and color of ginger, sweet potatoes, cashews, and coconut milk he sees for sale at a market.

◗ Media and Film

Malaysia has dozens of newspapers. The main newspaper, *Berita Harian,* is in Malay, but newspapers are also published in English (*New Straits Times*), Chinese, and Tamil. Malaysian radio and television programs are also broadcast in the country's major languages.

Malaysia has very strong censorship laws. Besides national security, the government is also concerned about protecting the popu-

Malaysia's best-known actress is **Michelle Yeoh.** Her most famous film is *Crouching Tiger, Hidden Dragon*, winner of the Academy Award for Best Foreign Language Film of 2000. The athletic star performed her own stunts in this action-packed martial arts film.

lation from what it considers harmful moral influences. Censors cut scenes that feature swearing or kissing from foreign television and films. Because of censorship, Internet publications, such as the news-reporting Web publication Malaysiakini.com, are the best source of independent news in Malaysia. Malaysia has close to 9 million Internet users.

Malaysia's film industry has been active since the 1930s. Director and actor P. Ramlee rose to success in the 1950s and went on to act in seventy films. He remains well known in Malaysia. The director Erma Fatima's 1999 film, *Perempuan Melayu Terakhir*, is a romantic tale of the search for cultural roots. Alan D'Cruz's documentary film, *Guardians of the Forest* (2001), looks into the plight of Malaysia's indigenous peoples and how a dam-building project changes the way of life for one group.

Women in ethnic Malay costumes demonstrate **weaving** techniques at the Sarawak Cultural Village in Sarawak, Malaysia.

The Arts

Many of the traditional arts of Malaysia—batik, for example—are made with cloth. Malaysians also excel in the art of weaving. Especially in the states of Kelantan and Terengganu, weavers make elaborate fabrics called *kain songket* on looms in the home. Gold or silver threads form geometric designs in these beautiful fabrics. Clothing made from kain songket is worn on special occasions.

Other arts that distinguish Malaysia are created from the raw materials that are abundant in the country. The Orang Asli of the peninsula carve hardwoods into expressive figures of animals and supernatural beings. Woodcarving is also a highly developed art among the people of Sarawak, who are famous for detailed, abstract representations of the hornbill bird. Entire tree trunks used to be carved into burial columns for chiefs. Baskets, sleeping mats, seats, and building materials for longhouses are woven from forest materials such as rattan, bamboo, and swamp grasses. Metalworking has long been a special craft of the people of the tin-rich peninsula, and residents of Selangor and Perak make handsome pewter (a mixture of tin and lead) items.

Traditional Malaysian architecture is both functional and beautiful. The high-pitched roof of a kampong house may be covered with clay tiles, corrugated zinc, or atap (sewn panels of palm branches). In another traditional architectural style, Minangkabau, the roof flares upward at both ends and resembles ox horns. For decoration, the house may have elaborate wooden grillwork under its eaves and an ornately tiled set of stairs.

Big cities in Malaysia are full of modern architecture, including gleaming glass high-rise buildings. The Petronas Towers are an architectural symbol of modern Malaysia. Their five-tiered structure reflects the five pillars of Islam, the guiding principles of Islam. The towers rise gracefully to crowns like the minarets, or towers, of mosques.

Music and Dance

Islamic and Chinese musical styles influence much of the modern music that Malaysians enjoy. Islamic chants called *hadrah* are sometimes accompanied by dance. Chinese-influenced romantic songs called *dondang sayang* are accompanied by an orchestra. A wide range of Western music styles are also important influences, in spite of the objections of some Muslim fundamentalists who believe that Western music is an immoral influence. Rock and pop singers perform in the nation's many nightclubs. A number of Western-style musicians have gained popularity in Malaysia. Sheila Majid is a popular jazz singer. Too Phat is a Malaysian hip-hop band, and the group Search plays heavy

Joe Flizzow *(left)* and Malique of the Malaysia hip-hop group Too Phat perform at a club in Singapore in 2004.

metal. The Malaysian Philharmonic Orchestra performs in a space in KL's Petronas Towers.

Percussion instruments, especially the *gendang* (drum), are the main instruments of traditional Malaysian music. Other percussion instruments are made of shells, coconuts, bamboo, and wood. Malaysian musicians also perform traditional Indonesian gamelan music, an orchestra of gongs, xylophones, and a drum. Perhaps the most unusual traditional music in Malaysia comes from Sarawak, where musicians play the guitarlike *sape*—as well as gongs, drums, and bamboo flutes—to produce a highly rhythmic sound.

Traditional dances are performed on special occasions such as weddings by professional dancers. In Kuala Lumpur, the Petronas Performing Arts Group presents more than one hundred dances. Dance dramas, performed with masks, take place at certain Buddhist temples.

Sports and Recreation

Malaysians are fond of sports, and they participate in a variety of sports. Some games are native to the country, and others originated in Great Britain and North America. Of Malaysian sports, *sepak takraw* (Malay football) is the best known. In this game, similar to a combination of volleyball and soccer, players use their feet or heads to knock a lightweight ball made of rattan (interwoven palm stems) back and forth across a net. Top spinning and kite flying are competitive sports, not children's games, in Malaysia. Horse racing draws avid fans, with five world-class tracks in the nation.

Of the imported sports, soccer is by far the most popular. Many schools compete, and rivalries are intense. Soccer teams represent each of the Malaysian states as well as the armed forces. The teams compete annually in a regional tournament with the nations of Singapore and Brunei.

Badminton is another of Malaysia's leading sports. Malaysian teams have often won the Thomas Cup—the symbol of international badminton competition—and gone to the Olympic Games. The game remains extremely popular and, along with basketball, field hockey, and cricket, attracts many enthusiasts. The fast-paced ball-and-racquet game squash is another Malaysian favorite.

Holidays and Festivals

Different states have local holidays, but all Malaysia celebrates its 1957 independence on National Day, August 31. Malaysia's different ethnic communities honor different holidays throughout the year. Chinese and Hindu calendars are based on the lunar (moon)

At the 2002 Asian Games in South Korea, Malaysia plays South Korea in the **sepak takraw semifinals.** Nasaruddin Mohamad Azman of Malaysia *(right)* blocks the ball from South Korea's Yoo Dong Young.

cycles, and the Muslim calendar has only 354 days in a year, so holiday dates vary each year.

During the month of Ramadan, Muslim's do not eat or drink anything from sunrise to sunset, in honor of Allah's revelation of the Quran to Muhammad. Hari Raya Puasa marks the end of Ramadan and is a public holiday. Muslims buy new clothes, clean their homes, and visit friends and family at this joyful time.

Chinese New Year in late January is a time for Chinese family reunions, dragon and lion dances, and firecrackers. Celebrations go on for fifteen days. The Lantern Festival in September honors the full moon, with moon viewings and baked sweets called moon cakes.

Hindus worship many gods who appear in many forms. This shrine in the Batu Caves honors the **Hindu god Ganesha** in the form of an elephant. He is the Lord of success, the destroyer of obstacles, and the god of education, knowledge, wisdom, and wealth.

Malaysia's Indian Hindu community celebrates Diwali, the Festival of Lights, in the fall. People light tiny oil lamps outside their home to invite Lakshmi, the goddess of wealth, to enter. The festival of Thaipusam draws the largest gathering in multiracial Malaysia, as non-Hindus also participate in this lively festival of thanksgiving and hope. Malaysian Christians observe Christmas on December 25 as a time for family, friends, and feasting.

◉ Food

Malaysia's abundant fresh vegetables and tropical fruits, spices, seafood, and rich ethnic traditions provide the ingredients for delicious Malaysian cuisine. Typical Malay dishes include *satays* (grilled meat on skewers in spicy peanut sauce), fried tofu (soybean curd) in peanut sauce, sweet-sour tamarind fish curry, spicy hot curry shrimps, and flavorful curried meats in coconut-milk sauce. Traditional seasonings include limes, lemongrass, cumin, cardamom, cloves, cinnamon, and star anise. A paste of hot chilies mixed with various seasonings accompanies most meals.

Traditional forest foods of Borneo include boiled roots of cassava (also called manioc or tapioca), tender bamboo shoots, fresh green fern tips, and roasted wild pig.

Rice or noodles are staples of the Malaysian diet. Religious law forbids Muslims to eat pork. Many Buddhists and Hindus are vegetarian. A traditional everyday meal consists of rice, a spicy meat or seafood dish, and flavorful vegetable dishes. Up to six dishes are placed on the table at the same time for everyone to share. In popular banana leaf restaurants, a green banana leaf serves as a plate for curries and spicy vegetable dishes.

A wide variety of fruit juices—including coconut juice drunk from the coconut—are refreshing drinks available everywhere. Coffee and tea are served hot or cold with generous amounts of milk and sugar. Islam forbids drinking alcohol, but locally brewed cold beer is popular with many Malaysians. Yogurt drinks help diners cool their mouths when eating spicy meals. Fresh fruit is often served as dessert. Sweets include cakes and concoctions made of rice and coconut. Malaysians also enjoy *cendol* (sugar syrup, coconut milk, and green noodles) and *ais kacang* (beans and fruit-flavored gelatin topped with shaved ice, colored syrups, and condensed milk).

RUJAK MEDAN (SPICY FRUIT SALAD)

If you can't find all these tropical fruits, you can substitute other fruits. Some, such as pineapple, can be bought canned. Tamarind paste, from the tamarind tree pod, is available at Asian food stores. Be careful handling hot chilies—their juice can burn skin. The tangy sauce is similar to satay sauce. Put in half the sugar, and try serving it with grilled meats or vegetables.

Fruit Salad:

1 Asian pear, sliced

1 small cucumber, peeled, seeded, and sliced

1 small jicama, peeled and cubed

1 firm, ripe papaya or mango, peeled and cubed

1 star fruit (carambola), sliced into star shapes

2 cups cubed pineapple

2 kiwifruits, peeled and sliced

Sauce:

2 tablespoons peanut butter

1 hot chili, seeded and sliced

1 inch fresh gingerroot, peeled and sliced

½ cup brown sugar

¼ cup tamarind paste, dissolved in ½ cup warm water and strained

2 tablespoons soy sauce

1 tablespoon lime juice

1 banana, peeled

1. Prepare fruit. Give yourself plenty of time for all the peeling and chopping.
2. In a blender, mix all sauce ingredients to form a smooth paste.
3. Gently mix fruit and sauce together, and serve in individual bowls. Serve at room temperature for full flavor.

Serves 6

THE ECONOMY

In the years after independence, Malaysia enjoyed one of the world's fastest-growing economies. The nation's success drew on its wealth of natural resources, its well-educated population, and the move to a diversified economy. Once dependent on agricultural products such as rubber and palm oil, Malaysia became a giant in manufacturing exports, especially electronics. As industry grew, large numbers of people moved to cities for higher-paying jobs in industry and other opportunities. Small farms were developed into more productive large plantations. Government agencies sponsored improvements that include large irrigation and drainage systems, new farm machinery (especially power tillers), and breeds of crops that produce higher yields. The country developed and produced its own automobile, the Proton. New towns were built, and standards of living increased around the country.

However, the 1997 Asian financial crisis brought Malaysia's economic growth to a halt. The value of the country's currency and stock market dropped dramatically. Malaysia's economy stabilized fairly quickly.

In the twenty-first century, Malaysia's economy is experiencing moderate growth again, with the successful electronics industry leading the way. Unemployment is a very low 3 percent, and inflation is also low at less than 2 percent.

Services and Tourism

The service sector of the economy provides services rather than producing goods and merchandise. Malaysia's service sector—including jobs in government, health services, education, retail, and tourism—produces 59 percent of the GDP (gross domestic product, the value of the goods and services produced by a country in one year). A little more than 49 percent of the working population is employed in service work.

Malaysia is a popular destination for tourists from Singapore, Australia, China, India, and Japan, and the country's tourist industry is growing rapidly, with more than 10 million visitors annually. With natural beauty, excellent public services, and a largely English-speaking population, Malaysia also draws tourists from North America and Europe. Malaysia promotes itself as a destination for rain forest safaris, river trips, and mountain treks. National parks serve two purposes—attracting tourists who want to see the rain forest and protecting the natural habitat, the people, and the wildlife that live there.

Catch up on the latest news about Malaysia's economy. You'll find links at www.vgsbooks.com.

Industry, Mining, and Petroleum

Malaysia's industrial sector, which includes manufacturing and mining, provides 34 percent of the GDP. Jobs in the industrial sector employ 36 percent of the labor force.

Because prices for its raw materials often fluctuate depending on the world demand, Malaysia, under Mahathir's guidance, decided to broaden its industrial economy. The nation developed many industries so that sudden price drops for a single commodity would not significantly damage the national economy. This diversification has proved very successful.

The electronic industry has brought Malaysia the greatest success. The country is one of the world's leading producers of computer disk drives. The island of Penang is the center of Malaysia's high-tech industry, and Penang offers research and development to meet the computer needs of computer companies around the world. Malaysia's rubber products industry uses its own rubber output to make tires, shoes, medical supplies, and other manufactured goods.

In the early 1980s, the Malaysian government promoted the development of a national auto industry. Malaysia's Proton Saga went into production in 1985, and Proton dominates the domestic car market in Malaysia. In 1996 Proton bought the British carmaker Lotus.

Mining makes up 40 percent of Malaysia's industrial earnings. About four-fifths of this comes from petroleum production. Petroleum products—crude oil and natural gas—became Malaysia's most profitable export in the late 1970s. Malaysia has two main oil-producing regions, one off the coast of Sarawak and Sabah and the other off the eastern coast of West Malaysia. In both of these regions, drilling rigs must be anchored in the ocean floor to extract the petroleum. More than thirty oil fields are in production around the country.

At the Malaysian automaker **Proton's factory in Shah Alam,** inspectors assess a Proton Waja as it comes off the assembly line.

An agency of the Malaysian government, PETRONAS supervises all exploration, drilling, and processing of petroleum products. It also decides which international firms may participate in Malaysia's business and undertakes international exploration as well. As part of its effort to become a more industrialized country, Malaysia has built five oil refineries and other factories to process the by-products of petroleum.

Tin, once the most important natural resource on the Malay Peninsula, is now a far less significant part of Malaysia's economy. Tin mining accounts for less than 3 percent of total output, and Malaysia has fallen to become the world's eighth-largest tin producer. Tin mining continues, however, especially in the states of Selangor and Perak. Tin dredges (earth-scooping machines) operate in Malaysia's large open-pit mines, and many other small mines operate as well.

West Malaysia also mines iron ore and bauxite (the raw material for making aluminum), and Sabah has a copper mine. These minerals, however, do not play a major part in Malaysia's economy. Other mineral resources that exist in small amounts are coal, antimony (a brittle metal used in alloys), and gold.

◎ Agriculture

The agricultural sector, including forestry and fishing, accounts for 7 percent of Malaysia's GDP. Agriculture employs almost 15 percent of the country's workers. The main agricultural products are palm oil, timber, rubber, rice, cacao beans, tropical fruits, pepper, shrimp, and other seafood.

Oranges are one of many fruits Malaysians grow. The fruit evolved in Southeast Asia millions of years ago, and traders spread the highly successful commercial fruit tree around the world. The color of an orange's skin has nothing to do with how ripe the fruit is inside. Oranges only turn orange in climates where it gets cool at night. In always-warm Malaysia, oranges are an emerald green when they are ripe.

Rice is Malaysia's main subsistence crop (grown for local consumption), but production meets only 71 percent of the nation's needs. Consequently, rice must be imported. If Malaysia used its land for more crops for domestic consumption, it could feed its people. But the government believes that the country's long-term prosperity depends on moneymaking export crops and importing much of its food.

Malaysia's forests provide three of the nation's most important exports: palm oil, timber, and rubber. The country is the largest manufacturer of palm oil in the world, producing 62 percent of the world's supply.

Oil palms are stout trees that bear bunches of a reddish brown, nutlike fruit that contain a vegetable oil used in dozens of different

Immigrant Thai women **harvest rice** in Tumpat, Kelantan, Malaysia.

products. Cosmetics, margarine, and even lightweight fuels and lubricants contain palm oil. When profits from rubber fell, many Malaysian farmers cut down their rubber trees and replanted their fields with oil palms.

Malaysia is a storehouse of timber, including tropical hardwoods such as mahogany, ebony, and teak. Fragrant sandalwood and camphor are also valuable forest woods. Logging is a major business, especially in the states of Sarawak and Sabah. Sarawak produces 62 percent of total production, Sabah produces 12 percent, and West Malaysia, 26 percent. Tropical logging is not sustainable, however, and it is estimated that Sabah may run out of marketable timber. Rapid logging does not allow old growth forests to grow back. Once the old trees are gone, the soil washes away and trees cannot grow there. Malaysia's government began a forest replantation program in 1995 to guarantee a sustainable future for Malaysia's timber industry, but environmentalists remain concerned at the loss of forest.

Although rubber is a significant export, its importance to Malaysia's economy has steadily declined since the development of synthetic (chemically made) rubber. Thailand, Indonesia, and Malaysia together produce 85 percent of the world's rubber. Malaysia remains the world's third-largest natural rubber producer.

Cocoa production is Malaysia's fourth most important agricultural moneymaker after palm oil, timber, and rubber. Malaysia's other export crops include tropical fruits, coconuts, tea, coffee, and cassava. Sarawak produces 11 percent of the world's supply of pepper, the world's fifth-largest producer. Grown on small plots, pepper bushes produce small, green berries that are dried in the sun until they become hard peppercorns.

BIRD'S NEST SOUP

Malaysia is the world's second-largest supplier of edible bird's nests, after Indonesia. Swiftlets—sparrow-sized birds—weave cuplike nests from strands of their gluey saliva that sticks to cave walls. Chinese people have been eating these nests for hundreds of years. Cooks prepare the tasteless nests in chicken broth. This soup is believed to be healthy, and diners in places like Hong Kong pay almost sixty dollars per bowl. To gather the nests, nest collectors balance on bamboo poles to reach the nests. This dangerous occupation is traditionally passed down from father to son. Modern methods cultivate the birds in houses. After the nests are removed from the caves or houses, they are washed before being shipped for domestic and international sale. Malaysia's bird's nest industry is a multimillion-dollar enterprise.

Tropical fruit production has expanded in the twenty-first century. Malaysia is about 90 percent self-sufficient in fruits and vegetables. Fruits grown for export include bananas, papayas, pineapples, watermelons, star fruits, mangoes, and more. The main fruits grown for local consumption are durian and bananas. Durian is a football-sized fruit covered with hard spikes. Inside is creamy, sweet flesh that gives off an incredibly stinky odor.

Some Malaysian farmers raise livestock. The country is largely self-sufficient in poultry, pork, and eggs and exports these foods, mostly to Singapore. Malaysia imports beef and mutton (meat from sheep).

Malaysia's per person consumption of fish is the highest in Southeast Asia. Despite its extensive coastlines, Malaysia imports about 10 percent of the fish its citizens eat. Aquaculture, or fish farming, has extended rapidly, but 85 percent of the fish catch comes from the sea. Malaysian fishers catch fish such as anchovies and mackerel from coastal waters. Shrimp is Malaysia's main seafood export.

Transportation and Energy

An important factor in Malaysia's economic growth has been its high-quality infrastructure—the system of roads, electrical power lines, telephone networks, and other basic public services. Malaysia has about 58,500 miles (94,000 km) of roads, and about 75 percent of them are paved. Roads are very congested, as most middle-class Malaysians own cars. Motorcycles and motor scooters provide less expensive transportation. Buses provide public transportation. In 1995, to ease urban traffic jams, Kuala Lumpur installed a light-rail system that operates electric trains.

Passengers wait to board a **light-rail train** in Kuala Lumpur.

The railway system in West Malaysia dates from 1931. Sabah has a rail service that extends southward from Kota Kinabalu, but Sarawak has no railway. Flights of the government-owned Malaysian Airlines link these Bornean states to the rest of the nation and provide Malaysia with an international air network as well. Flying is often the best way to travel in Malaysia's mountainous and forested terrain, and the country has 117 airports, 38 of which are paved. KL's international airport opened in 1998.

Waterways also remain important means of transportation, especially in the interior of the country. Malaysia is linked to international shipping by the Strait of Malacca on the west and the South China Sea to the east. International ports such as Melaka are continually being improved.

Malaysia has ample supplies of energy sources. Oil, natural gas, and electricity from dams that harness the power of rushing water meet the country's energy needs. Electricity from hydroelectric and gas-burning plants reaches almost every settlement in West Malaysia as well as the cities of the East Malaysia. Malaysia's public utilities are among the best in Asia, and most Malaysians enjoy basic services that are superior to those in most of the developing world.

The Future

Malaysia faces several serious challenges as it looks to the future. The needs of Malaysia's developing economy and growing population are sometimes out of balance with the need to protect the environment, particularly the disappearing rain forests. The government also strives to maintain a stable balance among people of different religions, ethnic groups, and income levels.

Though Malaysia's aim to raise the level of bumiputras' economic status has not quite hit its target, the general success of offering special privileges to these ethnic groups has led to a relaxation of the policy. In the twenty-first century, Prime Minister Abdullah and some other Malay politicians are calling for a total end to special privileges for ethnic Malays. Abdullah pointed out that bumiputras own 23 percent of Malaysia's businesses and that the time has come to encourage open competition.

Abdullah's government is pledged to follow Mahathir's policies of working toward ethnic harmony in the diverse country, guiding Malaysia's economy toward full industrial development, and encouraging democracy. With the country's wealth of natural resources, developing industries, and an educated and healthy population, Malaysia is well positioned to face the challenges of the twenty-first century.

CA. 50,000 B.C. Early Stone Age people are living around the Niah Caves in Sarawak.

CA. 2000 B.C. Late Stone Age people (Proto-Malays) with complex stone tools arrive in Malaysia.

CA. 250 B.C. More immigrants come to Malaysia, bringing metalworking knowledge.

A.D. 100s Indian merchants develop trading centers along the western coast of the Malay Peninsula. Malays begin to adopt Indian culture.

CA. 600 The Sumatran Sri Vijaya Empire begins to extend its influence over the Malay Peninsula. This trading empire brings the Buddhist religion.

CA. 1180s Some Chinese merchants begin to live permanently in West Malaysia.

1403 Prince Paramesvara of Sumatra establishes his rule at Melaka and soon builds the city into a thriving and powerful port city.

1445 Muzaffar Shah, a local Malay leader, becomes sultan (ruler) of Melaka and makes Islam the territory's official religion.

1511 A well-armed Portuguese fleet captures Melaka from the Malays.

1600 British traders establish the British East India Company (BEIC) for trade in Asia.

1641 The Dutch seize Melaka from the Portuguese.

1786 The British establish a naval station (modern-day George Town) and trading facilities on Penang Island.

1819 Stamford Raffles from the BEIC selects Singapore as the site for a new trading center.

1826 The BEIC combines Melaka, Penang, and Singapore into the Straits Settlements.

1841 The sultan of Brunei grants James Brooke the title of raja (prince) of Sarawak.

1868 Yap Ah Loy becomes the Kapitan China, or leader of the Chinese, in the fast-growing tin-mining town of Kuala Lumpur.

1877 The British introduce the rubber tree from Brazil to Malaysia.

1881 Trading rights on Sabah (North Borneo) go to the British North Borneo Company, which administers Sabah for the British government.

1913 All of modern-day Malaysia is under British rule and loosely united in a federation called British Malaya.

1931 The Chinese population of British Malaya numbers 1.7 million, and the native Malay population numbers 1.6 million. The British encourage ethnic groups to be separate.

1942   The Japanese fully occupy Malaya and rule from Singapore.

1948   The British establish the Federation of Malaya, keeping Malays in
        political power and limiting non-Malay citizenship. Chinese Communist
        guerrillas resist British rule, sparking the Emergency.

1957   The Federation of Malaya achieves *merdeka* (independence), with Tunku Abdul
        Rahman as the new nation's first prime minister.

1963   Singapore, Sarawak, and Sabah join the new nation and become part of the newly
        named independent Federation of Malaysia.

1969   The ethnic riots in Kuala Lumpur lead to the death of hundreds.

1971   The government introduces the New Economic Policy (NEP) to create a better
        balance of economic power among the nation's ethnic groups.

1981   Mahathir Mohamed becomes Malaysia's prime minister. He is a proponent of
        special privileges for bumiputras.

1985   Malaysia's first car, the Proton Saga, goes into production.

1989   The Islamic Family Law of 1989 gives Muslim women more legal rights in family
        matters.

1992   Mahathir outlines his Vision 2020 plan, calling for Malaysia to be a fully developed country
        by the year 2020.

1994   The government bans al-Arqam, an Islamic sect, claiming it preaches militant Islam.

1995   Construction begins on the Petronas Towers in Kuala Lumpur, once the world's tallest
        building.

1997   An Asian financial crisis brings Malaysia's economic growth to a halt.

2001   Terrorists strike the United States, and Mahathir pledges to fight global terrorism.

2002   Harsh new laws against illegal immigrants cause a human rights crisis when 300,000
        workers are forced to leave Malaysia.

2003   Prime Minister Mahathir resigns after twenty-two years. Abdullah Badawi becomes
        the new prime minister. English is reintroduced as a language of instruction in schools.

2004   A tsunami, or massive ocean wave, hits parts of Southeast Asia. Deaths
        in Malaysia are in the dozens but are many tens of thousands in
        neighboring Indonesia.

2005   A roundup of illegal immigrants again forces the departure of migrant work-
        ers. Some leaders call for an end to special privileges for bumiputras.

Currency Fast Facts

COUNTRY NAME Malaysia

AREA 127,320 square miles (329,758 sq. km)

MAIN LANDFORMS Malay Peninsula, Borneo, Crocker Range, Bintang Range, Mount Tahan Range, Timor Range, Titi Wangsa Range

HIGHEST POINT Mount Kinabalu (13,431 feet, or 4,094 meters)

LOWEST POINT Sea level

MAJOR RIVERS Rajang, Kinabatangan, Pahang, Kelantan, Perak

ANIMALS Ants, Asian elephants, bat hawks, bats, butterflies, civet cats, cobras, crested serpent eagles, crocodiles, deer, flying foxes, flying snakes, flying squirrels, geckos, herons, hornbills, leopards, monitor lizards, monkeys, moon moths, mosquitoes, orangutans, otters, pangolins, proboscis monkeys, pythons, sandpipers, sea turtles, storks, sun bears, tapirs, termites, tigers, two-horned rhinoceroses, vipers, wild oxen, wild pigs

CAPITAL CITY Kuala Lumpur is the legislative capital. Putrajaya is the administrative capital.

OTHER MAJOR CITIES Ipoh, Johor Baharu, Melaka, Kota Kinabalu, George Town, Kuching

OFFICIAL LANGUAGE Bahasa Malaysia

MONETARY UNIT ringgit (RM). 100 sen = 1 ringgit

MALAYSIAN CURRENCY

The ringgit is sometimes called the Malaysian dollar. Bills (paper money) come in ringgit denominations of 1, 2, 5, 10, 20, 50, 100, 500, and 1,000. Coins come in sen values of 1, 5, 10, 20, and 50. The first king of Malaysia and the hibiscus flower are on all ringgit bills. Depictions of Malaysia's economic accomplishments, such as the Petronas Towers, illustrate most bills. Coins carry depictions of Malaysian cultural items, such as a kite and a *keris* (traditional dagger).

Malaysia's national flag has fourteen horizontal red and white stripes, representing the thirteen states and the federal government. A dark blue square in the upper quarter next to the staff stands for the unity of Malaysia's different peoples. A crescent moon inside the square is the symbol of Islam. Next to the moon, a star with fourteen points symbolizes the unity of the thirteen states and the federal government. The yellow color of the moon and the star is the royal color of Malaysia's rulers.

"Negaraku" or "Negara Ku," "My Country" is the national anthem of Malaysia. The song was chosen as a national anthem in 1957 after the Federation of Malaya's independence from Britain. The tune was borrowed from a well-known and popular Malay song titled "Terang Bulan," or "Bright Moon," which was the state anthem of Perak at the time. Perak was the first state to have an anthem, and it gained one in an unusual way. When a member of the Perak royal family was invited to a formal event in Europe, he was asked what his state anthem was. But his state didn't have an anthem. In order to appear dignified, he proceeded to hum his favorite popular tune, and it later became the official state anthem. The following is an English translation of the anthem.

Negaraku (My Country)
My country, my native land.
The people living united and progressive,
May God bestow blessing and happiness.
May our Ruler have a successful reign.
May God bestow blessing and happiness.
May our Ruler have a successful reign.

Listen to Malaysia's national anthem. Visit www.vgsbooks.com for a link.

Note: Muslim Malays are usually known by their personal first name. Traditional Chinese names put the family name first, in reverse order of Western names.

ABDULLAH AHMAD BADAWI (b. 1939) Prime Minister Abdullah was born in Penang. His father was a founding member of Malaysia's ruling party, UMNO. His college degree is in Islamic studies. Elected to parliament in 1978, Abdullah served in his country's defense, foreign affairs, and education ministries. When Prime Minister Mahathir retired in October 2003, Abdullah succeeded him. He promised to continue Mahathir's policies, to oversee Malaysia's vibrant economy, and to stamp out widespread political corruption. In March 2004, Abdullah's coalition government won a landslide victory in country-wide elections. He faces political challenges from opposition Islamic fundamentalists. Because he is less charismatic and controversial than Mahathir, some Malaysians call Abdullah Mr. Nice Guy.

CHOONG HANN WONG (b. 1977) Choong is a badminton player from Kuala Lumpur. He was the first Malaysian to play in the men's singles finals of the World Badminton Championships, and he competed at the 2004 Summer Olympics in Athens, Greece. Pursuing his undergraduate studies in business, he also promotes the game of badminton by participating as a coach in badminton clinics for secondary school students.

NICOL DAVID (b. 1985) David is a squash superstar from Penang who enjoys a very strong following in Southeast Asia. Squash is a fast-paced ball-and-racquet game. Some sports observers consider David the best Malaysian athlete ever. In 2005 she became the first Malaysian player to win the Malaysian Women's Open Squash Championship, when she beat world champion Vanessa Atkinson of the Netherlands. Malaysians are hopeful that the Olympic committee will add squash to the 2012 Olympic Games, because David's youth and skill will make her a favorite for a medal.

ANANDA KRISHNAN (b. 1938) Krishnan is Malaysia's second-richest businessperson, worth an estimated $3.2 billion. While avoiding public exposure, he is known to most Malaysians as the man who built the Petronas Towers, one of the world's tallest buildings. He was born in Kuala Lumpur's Little India neighborhood. Krishnan attended Harvard University for a master's in business administration in 1964. His business interests incorporate entertainment, space, oil, power, shipping, telecommunications, property, and legal gambling. Krishnan is a close friend of Malaysia's ex-prime minister, Mahathir.

MAHATHIR MOHAMAD (b. 1925) Prime minister of Malaysia for twenty-two years, Mahathir was Asia's longest-serving elected ruler. Born in Alor Setar, Kedah, Mahathir is a doctor by training. He wrote *The Malay Dilemma* in 1970 and came to power as an advocate of special privileges for Malays. He also promoted the status of women. Mahathir became prime minister in 1981. He successfully guided Malaysia in economic development, a policy that brought him great popularity. He also maintained relative peace and stability in the multiethnic, multireligion country. However, Mahathir's authoritarian rule also suppressed free speech and denied some groups' equal rights. Known for his outspoken, often anti-Western views, Mahathir retired in 2003 as prime minister. Since retiring, he has been serving as an adviser to several corporations, including PETRONAS. Mahathir's wife, Hamsah, is also a physician, and they have seven children.

ALLAHYARHAM USMAN AWANG (1929–2001) Born in Kuala Sedili, Johor, Usman was Malaysia's National Poet Laureate, or poet of special honor. Writing under the name Tongkat Waran, he published more than two hundred poems. A champion of the use of the Malay language, Usman also wrote plays and literary criticism. Known as a humanist, his work bridges the gulf of ethnic and religious differences in his homeland. His collection of poetry *Salam Benua* is available in English as *Greetings to the Continent*.

WAN AZIZAH ISMAIL (b. 1952) Wan Azizah is an ethnic Malay politician and leader of the Malay-majority Keadilan (People's Justice) Party. She holds a seat in parliament representing Penang's Permatang Pauh. She is married to Anwar Ibrahim, Malaysia's former deputy prime minister, and they have six children. Wan Azizah studied medicine in Ireland and became an ophthalmologist (eye doctor) but retired from her profession in 1993. Never politically outspoken before, she founded the Keadilan Party when her husband was arrested on charges of corruption in 1998. Keadilan is working to create an honest, democratic, Islamic government.

MICHELLE YEOH (b. 1962) Yeoh, originally named Yeoh Chu-Kheng, was born in Ipoh. Named Miss Malaysia in 1983, she went on to become one of Asia's top film stars. An athletic actor who performs her own stunts, Yeoh studied ballet in London and achieved her fame first in Hong Kong's film industry. She earned worldwide fame in the James Bond film *Tomorrow Never Dies* (1997) and the martial arts epic *Crouching Tiger, Hidden Dragon* (winner of four Academy Awards for 2000).

ZETI AKHTAR AZIZ (b. 1947) Born in Johor Bahru, Zeti is the head of the Bank of Malaysia, the nation's central bank, since 2000. Her father was the vice president of the University of Malaya. She received her Ph.D. from the University of Pennsylvania, as a specialist in financial policy. Her career with Malaysia's national bank began in 1985, and she was instrumental in helping Malaysia recover from the Asian financial crisis of 1997. Besides overseeing the nation's finances, she also writes and speaks around the world about economics.

BATU CAVES The Batu Caves are north of Kuala Lumpur. Temple Cave is a large cavern with a ceiling about 330 feet (100 m) tall. Visitors climb 272 steps, a feat performed by many Hindus on the way to the cave's shrine to offer prayers. The Gallery Cave displays art illustrating Hindu mythology. The Dark Cave is a network of caverns that cave animals inhabit. The Malaysian Nature Society operates spelunking (cave exploring) tours.

GEORGE TOWN Located on Penang Island, George Town has colonial architecture, famous Asian cuisine, and lively Chinatown and Little India neighborhoods to attract many tourists. The Temple of the Reclining Buddha houses a 108-foot (33 m) long Buddha in a golden robe. Indian Muslims built the yellow-domed Masjid Kapitan Keling mosque in 1801. Trishaws—three-wheeled bicycle taxis—are a good way to get around the winding historical streets. Nearby luxury beach resorts offer beautiful scenery and waterskiing or parasailing.

KELLIE'S CASTLE Eccentric British planter William Kellie Smith started to build this exotic, Moorish-style mansion in the forest near Ipoh in 1909. Local legend says it is haunted and has secret passages leading to hidden chambers. Maintained as a tourist site, the mansion is surrounded by a deer and bird park.

KUALA LUMPUR This city grew from a wild tin-mining town into a high-tech, modern capital. The gleaming Petronas Towers rise over the nineteenth-century KL Train Station, the pink- and cream-colored Masjid Jamek mosque, the kite-shaped National Theater, and many other sights. Merdeka (Independence) Square is in the heart of the historic colonial district. Chinatown is a bustling area with old painted shop-houses, temples, and a night market. Malaysia's history, arts and crafts, and culture are on display at the National Museum. Malaysia Fest, two weeks of celebration and performances in September, is a good time to visit.

SARAWAK MUSEUM, KUCHING Charles Brooke, nephew of the white raja James Brooke, founded this museum in 1888 along with biologist Alfred Russell Wallace. The result is the world's best collection of Borneo artistry and one of the best museums in Southeast Asia. Visitors can climb up into a reconstructed longhouse and examine early photographs and artifacts of longhouse life, including skull trophies.

SEMENGGOH WILDLIFE REHABILITATION CENTRE Located on Sarawak near the town of Kuching, this sanctuary rehabilitates orangutans, hornbills, monkeys, and bears that have been orphaned, injured, or illegally captured. The semiwild orangutans roam free, and visitors can see them during twice-daily feeding times when they return to the center. Nearby Kubah National Park offers walking tours of the rain forest that is the orangutans' natural habitat.

batik: a traditional method of hand-dying cloth with elaborate designs

colonial rule: control by a foreign power over a dependent area or people

Dayak: "person of the interior," the group name for the many different original peoples of Borneo. In the twenty-first century, some Dayaks live and work in modern cities.

deforestation: the loss of forests due to logging or clearing land for human uses. Deforestation leads to soil erosion, loss of wildlife habitat, and global warming.

global warming: the gradual increase in the average worldwide temperature of the earth's atmosphere, according to many scientists

gross domestic product (GDP): the value of the goods and services produced by a country in one year

guerrilla: a small group of fighters who operate independently and engage in nontraditional warfare, such as hit-and-run strikes

hunter-gatherer: a person who hunts animals and gathers wild plants for survival

hydroelectric power: electricity produced by damming a river and then harnessing the energy of rushing water at hydroelectric power stations

kampong: a native Malay village. Houses in kampongs are built on stilts to stay dry.

longhouse: a large dwelling where traditional Dayak people of Borneo live. Up to twenty families live together in one longhouse.

peninsula: a fingerlike portion of land jutting out into water, connected on one side to a larger piece of land

Sharia: Islamic law that governs all aspects of devout Muslims' life. Malaysia has special Islamic law courts. Only Muslim Malaysians are subject to the rulings of these courts.

strait: a narrow passageway of water connecting two larger bodies of water

tropical rain forest: a woodland that grows in areas with high annual rainfall. Rain forest treetops form a continuous canopy (roof), so the forest floor does not receive much sunlight.

yang di-pertuan agong: "supreme ruler" in Malay, also called the king. The king is elected to serve as Malaysia's head of state for five years and mainly has a ceremonial role.

Selected Bibliography

Barwise, J. M., and N. J. White. *A Traveller's History of Southeast Asia.* **New York: Interlink Books, 2002.**
The complex history, cultures, peoples, and scenery of Southeast Asia, including Malaysia, are introduced in this guide for readers (whether or not they are travelers). The authors believe that many people only know about Southeast Asia through U.S. movies about the Vietnam War (1957–1975), such as *Apocalypse Now*, and they set out to debunk stereotypes in this book.

BBC News. **2005.**
http://www.bbc.co.uk (2005)
The World Edition of the BBC (British Broadcasting Corporation) News is updated throughout the day, every day. The BBC is a source for comprehensive news coverage about Malaysia and also provides an in-depth country profile.

The Economist. **2005.**
http://www.economist.com (June 3, 2005)
A weekly British magazine available online or in print, the *Economist* provides in-depth coverage of international news, including Malaysia's political and economic news. The *Economist* also offers country profiles with relevant articles as well as some statistics at http://www.economist.com/countries.

The Europa World Year Book 2004. **London: Europa Publications, 2004.**
This publication provides comprehensive coverage of the recent political events, governments, and economies in countries around the world.

Leibo, Steven A. *East, Southeast Asia, and the Western Pacific.* **Harper's Ferry, WV: Stryker-Post Publications, 2004.**
A title in the annual World Today series, this book gives the historical background of the entire region and focuses on each country individually. Malaysia's history, government, society and culture, and economy are covered in moderate detail.

Osborne, Milton. *Exploring Southeast Asia: A Traveller's History of the Region.* **Crows Nest, AU: Allen & Unwin, 2002.**
A lively chronicle of the region including Malaysia, this book is illustrated with maps, diagrams, and photographs and includes histories of all the Southeast Asian nations. Osborne calls Southeast Asia, "a world that deserves exploration . . . [of its] rich past, its triumphs and its tragedies."

Population Reference Bureau. **2004.**
http://www.prb.org (June 2005)
PRB's annual statistics provide in-depth demographics on Malaysia's population, including birth and death rates, infant mortality rates, and other statistics relating to health, environment, education, employment, family planning, and more.

Richmond, Simon, Marie Cambon, Damian Harper, and Richard Watkins. *Malaysia, Singapore & Brunei.* **Footscray, AU: Lonely Planet, 2004.**

A comprehensive guide to Malaysia, this book covers it all, from the rain forest of Borneo to the sleek sophistication of Kuala Lumpur. Detailed maps, color photos, guides to food, manners, and language, and a brief overview of history round out this useful book. Lonely Planet also has a website for travelers at http://www.lonelyplanet,com/destinations/south_east_asia/malaysia/.

Stuart-Fox, Martin. *A Short History of China and Southeast Asia: Tribute, Trade, and Influence.* **Crows Nest, AU: Allen & Unwin, 2003.**

Two thousand years of Chinese relations with Malaysia and the rest of Southeast Asia are charted in this book. China was historically the main power in the area, and the author states that as Western influence in Southeast Asia is passing, this leaves "China the opportunity to regain its historical position of regional dominance."

U.S. Department of State, Bureau of East Asian and Pacific Affairs. *Background Note: Malaysia.* **January 2005.**
http://www.state.gov **(June 2005).**

The background notes of the U.S. State Department supply information about U.S. relations with Malaysia as well as a brief profile of the country's people, history, government, political conditions, economy, and more. The Department of State website also provides timely access to official travel and foreign policy information at http://www.state.gov.

The World Factbook. **April 21, 2005.**
http://www.odci.gov/cia/publications/factbook/geos/my.html **(June 2005).**

This site of the CIA (the U.S. Central Intelligence Agency) provides ample facts and figures on Malaysian geography, people, government, economy, communications, transportation, military, and transnational issues.

Aw, Tash. *The Harmony Silk Factory.* **New York: Riverhead Books, 2005.**
This novel tells the story of the mysterious Johnny Lim, a Chinese Malaysian, from three points of view: his son's, his wife's, and that of his only friend, an Englishman. Set during the Japanese invasion of Malaysia, the story gradually reveals the intertwined fate of the characters. Aw writes wonderfully of the Malaysian landscape and weather as if they too were characters.

Geras, Adèle. *Other Echoes.* **New York: David Fickling Books, 2005.**
In this novel for young adults, eighteen-year-old Flora, living in Great Britain, remembers her childhood in North Borneo (Sabah), where she was treated as an outsider. She also uncovered the secret of an old house there.

Gordon, Matthew. *Islam.* **Rev. ed. New York: Facts of File, 2001.**
This book is part of the World Religions series. It provides an overview of Islam, discussing the religion's history, basic beliefs, and the modern Islamic world. Illustrations and sidebars accompany the informative text.

Keadilan
http://www.keadilanrakyat.org/english/
The website of the People's Justice Party, or Keadilan, carries political news and special features. Keadilan's political goals include espousing "Islam as the religion of the Federation whilst ensuring that the rights of non-Muslims to freedom of religion and conscience are guaranteed."

Lim, Shirley Geok-lin. *Joss and Gold.* **New York, The Feminist Press, 2001.**
This novel is about clashes of Malaysian culture seen through one Chinese Malaysian woman's life. The main character, Li An, is an English literature teacher at the university in KL. Married to a traditional Chinese man and friends with Indian and Malay students, she falls in love with an American Peace Corps worker during the time of the 1969 elections and ethnic violence. The author, who was born in Melaka and lives in California, also wrote a memoir, *Among the White Moon Faces.*

Malaysiakini
http://www.malaysiakini.com
This is a Web publication that operates without government control and is not owned by any political party, unlike most of Malaysia's print and broadcast media. Launched in 1999, Malaysiakini.com offers news, opinions, editorials, features, and letters. Since its launch, the website has become the leading source of independent news and views on Malaysia.

McNair, Sylvia. *Malaysia.* **New York: Children's Press, 2002.**
Part of the Enchantment of the World series, this book is a resource for information about Malaysia's land, economy, culture, and history. Colorful photos and charts supplement facts and figures.

Further Reading and Websites

Muhammad Haji Salleh. *Beyond the Archipelago: Selected Poems.* Athens: Ohio University Center for International Studies, 1995.

This book selects many of the best poems by one of Malaysia's leading poets. The poems are published on one page in the original Malay and, on the facing page, translated into English by the poet. Titles include "night rain," "the boat builder," and "the forest's last day," about the destruction of the rain forest.

Munan, Heidi, and Foo Yuk Yee. *Malaysia.* New York: Benchmark Books, 2002.

This book is part of the Cultures of the World series. Well illustrated with photos and charts, information is presented about Malaysia's geography, history, government, economy, environment, and people.

Rowell, Jonathan. *Malaysia.* Austin, TX: Raintree Steck-Vaughn, 1997.

This book, part of the Economically Developing Countries series for younger readers, looks specifically at Malaysia's economic conditions. Quotes from Malaysians enliven the factual information.

Sisters in Islam
http://www.sistersinislam.org.my

This is the website of a group of Malaysian Muslim women committed to promoting the rights of women. Their mission statement reads: "Our mission is to promote an awareness of the true principles of Islam, principles that enshrine the concept of equality between women and men, and to strive towards creating a society that upholds the Islamic principles of equality, justice, freedom and dignity within a democratic state."

The Star
http://www. jaring.my/%7Estar/

One of Malaysia's English-language newspapers, updated daily online, the *Star* covers major events in Malaysia.

vgsbooks.com
http://www.vgsbooks.com

Visit vgsbooks.com, the home page of the Visual Geography Series®. You can get linked to all sorts of useful online information, including geographical, historical, demographic, cultural, and economic websites. The vgsbooks.com site is a great resource for late-breaking news and statistics.

Captions for photos appearing on cover and chapter openers:

Cover: Constructing the eighty-eight-story Petronas Towers in Kuala Lumpur cost $1.9 billion. At 1,510 ft. (460 m.), they were the tallest buildings in the world when they were completed in 1998. (A taller building, Tapei 101, opened in Taipei, Taiwan, in 2004.)

pp. 4–5 Bullock cart operators show off their finest vehicles in Melaka.

pp. 8–9 Mount Kinabalu (13,431 ft., or 4,094 m) is Malaysia's highest peak.

pp. 38–39 Pedestrians, mopeds, and buses compete for space on a street in Klang, Malaysia. Signs in Malay, English, and Chinese identify its shops to passersby.

pp. 46–47 To create a batik design such as this one, an artist paints or presses a wax design onto a piece of fabric, then dips the fabric into colored dye. The color will soak into the cloth everywhere except where the wax remains. The artist then scrapes off the wax, presses new wax designs onto the cloth, and dips it into a different dye. By repeating this several times, a batik artist blends colors and designs on the cloth.

pp. 58–59 A Malaysian worker tests computer monitors at a Samsung factory south of Kuala Lumpur. Samsung is a South Korean company.

Photo Acknowledgments
The images in this book are used with the permission of: © Lucinda Naylor, pp. 4–5, 19, 23, 38–39, 49, 56; © XNR Productions, pp. 6, 11; © A. Gasson/Art Directors, pp. 8–9; © Colin Conway/Art Directors, p. 13; PhotoDisc Royalty Free by Getty Images, p. 14; © age fotostock/SuperStock, pp. 15, 64; © Jane Sweeney/Art Directors, p. 16; © Free Agents Limited/CORBIS, p. 25; Library of Congress, p. 27 (LC-USZ62-108108); © Hulton-Deutsch Collection/CORBIS, p. 29; © Bettmann/CORBIS, pp. 30, 32; © SuperStock, Inc./SuperStock, p. 41; © J. Highet/Art Directors, p. 43; © TENGKU BAHAR/AFP/Getty Images, p. 45; © Christine Osborne/CORBIS, pp. 46–47; © Rukhsana Hamid/UPPA/ZUMA Press, p. 51; © Steve Vidler/SuperStock, p. 52; © BAZUKI MUHAMMAD/Reuters/CORBIS, p. 53; © Reuters/CORBIS, pp. 54, 61; © Richard Sobol/ZUMA Press, pp. 58–59; © Robert Fried Photography/www.robertfriedphotography.com, p. 62; Audrius Tomonis—www.banknotes.com, p. 68.

Front cover: © John Elk III. Back cover: NASA